Be The One
To Execute Your Trust

Maine-Patriot.com
3 Linnell Circle
Brunswick, Maine 04011

http://maine-patriot.com

BE THE ONE

There is always a Remedy!

We create our own remedy; no one can do it for us.

"Congress shall make no law ... abridging ... the right of the people ... to petition the government for a redress of grievances." — *1st. Amendment to the Constitution for the United States of America.*

BE THE ONE

The People's Credit

We are Secured Party Creditors of the United States.

"Congress shall have power ...To borrow money on the credit of (the people of) **the United States."**

— *Section 8, clause 2, of the Constitution for the United States.*

BE THE ONE

Be The One

To Execute Your Trust

Contents

BE THE ONE

1
Contracts Make The Law

"No State shall ... pass any ... law impairing the obligation of contracts..." — Section 10, clause 1, of the Constitution for the United States.

Contracts make the law. The only way an Act of government can be binding on us is if we contract with the government through that Act.

Contracts make the law. Everything that is going on in the United States today is based on the ten planks of the communist manifesto. We are communists whether we know it or not who must change in order to become free.

Every member of my world has the power of attorney over himself, over his legal person; he is competent to handle his own affairs.

It's all contract. You don't owe them any money unless you contract with them to pay it.

No contract; no obligation to perform.

For instance: My friend got a speeding ticket and he wrote on the front and back, *"No contract; No consent; Offer refused",* and mailed it in to the court.

If he receives any correspondence from the court, he will write them back and demand that they *prove their claim in writing, with law references,* that his handling of the ticket was wrong. They can't prove that he was **conducting commerce** at the time of the traffic stop.

Our word trumps theirs no matter what is said.

As long as we know who and what we are in the law we cannot loose. If they send me anything in the mail, I will return it *"Offer Refused"* - within three days - as per contract law. You have 3 days to refuse any *contract offer* of any kind. Know who and what you are in the law, so that you will know how to handle any situation they present to you.

To remove contracts that you know nothing about, rebut their silent presumptions by declaring your *true status in the law "and the truth shall set you free."* (John 8:32)

*It all begins with knowing who you are. Names are irrelevant; it's the **role you play** in their game, that counts.*

"I am not a *citizen* of the UNITED STATES Corporation, therefore I am not an *employee* of the UNITED STATES INC., who is subject to the statutes and regulations defined in the IRS code, which apply only to U.S. contract employees. I am 'Man'. I was created by God with dominion. The created is subject to the Creator and to nothing else."

John Doe was named by his parents.
JOHN DOE was named by the state.

John Doe is his **lawful** name.

JOHN DOE is his **legal** name - his **street** name - his **strawman** name - his **transmitting utility** name issued by the state.

John's all capitalized legal name is on his ***Record of Live Birth*** on which his ***Birth Certificate*** is based. Nobody knows where it actually is; it's a legal fiction. You have to have a name but you don't care what name they are calling you by.

"I am Man." (or "Woman" as the gender may be)

There are two kinds of law. God's law and man's law. Natural law and contract law.

JOHN DOE is a **presumption** of man's law - a strawman or 'man of straw' - it is bait. They have to get you to join their game to be under their law.

If you don't want to play their game - you don't have to go by their rules.

"I am 'Man' and I was created by God with dominion."

Logic is irrelevant in court; courts deal in **presumptions** which until rebutted stand.

Remove their **presumptions** by rebutting their contracts that really don't exist.

It all comes down to intent - no criminal intent, no crime.

It's a matter of liability. Who's assuming the liability for the claims that are being made?

Contract forms the law.

So where is the contract? Who's compelling me to perform in a contract? Provide the evidence that a contract exists. Provide the contract that I am being compelled to perform, in that all Capitalized name.

Anything after "Man" is a legal construct; it's a fiction.

Do you want the *legal person,* JOHN DOE, or do you want the *lawful man,* John Doe? There is a difference between these two names; these two persons.

Separate the names - for there are two of us.

Which capacity do you want me to be in? Which role do you want me to play? The role of the man? Or the legal fiction; the presumption?

Tell me what role you want me to play — and I will - or I won't — it's my choice.

BE THE ONE

2
Presumptions? or Facts?

The State operates on **presumptions**...
The Courts operate on **presumptions**...
   ... what binds me to their **presumptions**?

- Where's the contract?

- What obligations in the contract am I allegedly bound to perform?

- Did I agree to it?

- Was the contract valid?

- Was mutual consideration exchanged?

- What type of consideration was exchanged?

- What's in the contract that I am supposed to perform?

- Was I aware of the contract?

- Was the contract fully disclosed?

- Did I sign the contract with my autograph in wet ink?

Statutory laws are **public servant codes** for society's slaves - for employed agents of government. We're all **presumed** to be employees and servants of the state — *until we object!*

We're servants of God - students of the earth charged with earth's cultivation and care.

BE THE ONE

3
Trusts Defined

DEFINITION: trust, n. A fiduciary relationship regarding property subjecting the person with title to the property to equitable duties to manage the property for another's benefit; the confidence placed in a trustee, together with the trustee's obligations toward the property for the benefit of the beneficiary.

A trust arises as a manifestation of an intent to create it. — Black's Law, 7th, page 1513.

Hence the ***Declarations of Independence*** of 1776 and 2012.

A trust involves three elements:

1. the trustee who holds title to the trust property and is subject to equitable duties to manage it for the benefit of another person according to a set plan;

2. the beneficiary to whom the trustee owes equitable duties to manage the trust property for his benefit;

3. trust property which is held in trust by the trustee for the beneficiary - called the **"corpus"** (corps) of the trust.

In the *wide sense,* a trust exists when property is to be held and administered by one person on behalf of another person according to established terms, or for some purpose other than the person's own benefit.

In the *narrow sense*... a trust exists when the creator of the trust hands over (*or is bound to hand over*) the control of an asset which is to be administered by another person (*the trustee*) (*the administrator in his capacity as such*) for the benefit of some person other than the trustee (*the beneficiary*) or for some impersonal purpose.

4

The Holy Trinity is Trust Law

God's Law entails a ***three party contract*** between ***Our Father*** (*God*), who operates through ***His Spirit*** (*the Holy Ghost*), for the benefit of ***His Son*** (Jesus the Christ) (*the earthly Grantor of the rights of all mankind*).

Corporate Law entails a ***three party contract*** between the ***Directors*** who direct their ***Employees*** for the benefit of the ***Stockholders***.

Trust Law entails a ***three party contract*** between the ***Executor*** who directs his ***Trustees*** for the benefit of the ***Beneficiaries***.

The actions are the same. Only the word definitions change for each case.

Picture a triangle . . .

Let the triangle represent the ***Trinity of the Bible*** (God's Law) — the ***Father***, the ***Son***, and the ***Holy Ghost***.

Picture the ***Father*** at the top of the *Triangle of His power and grace*.

Picture the ***Holy Ghost*** at the ***right hand*** point of the base, and ***God's Son*** at the ***left hand*** point of the base.

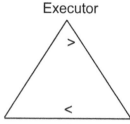

Our Father
Chief Executive Officer
Executor

God's Son   God's Spirit
Jesus, the Christ   **The Holy Ghost**
Beneficiary   Trustee

Power flows clockwise from **Our Father** (*God*) who operates through **His Spirit** (*the Holy Ghost*) for the benefit of **His Son** (*Jesus, the Christ*) who dispenses God's *mutually abundant* Grace to us all.

The Bible is God's Last Will and Testament.
A Testament is something left by a testator in a will.

There are **three parties** to a testament (a will).

The **executor**, the **beneficiary**, and the **trustee** who holds and manages the property *in trust* for the beneficiary.

The trustee is directed by the executor, according to the will (the constitution) of the trust, for the benefit of the beneficiary.

The Testator created the *Earth Trust* and put us in charge as the **executors** and *beneficiaries* of his will. What the Testator left us is being held and managed by our trustees supposedly for our benefit.

5

Trust Law Applied

According to trust law, the **executor** and the **beneficiary** cannot be a **trustee**, and a **trustee** cannot be the **executor** or the **beneficiary**.

The **trustee** must follow the terms of the trust. The **executor/beneficiary** establishes the terms of the trust. The **executor** gives directives to the **trustees** according to the terms of the trust for the benefit of the **beneficiaries**.

Government employees are our **public servants** who are supposed to be **trustees of the public trust** - but they are not. They hold and manage all **public property** for the benefit of *the state* instead of for the benefit of *the people* - you and me.

In court, if they send you to jail, it is because you were seen as a trustee who had been ordered to do something for a beneficiary that you did not do. You can't be a trustee and a beneficiary at the same time. Somebody else was supposed to get a benefit that they did not get because of what you did not do.

When you walk into court, you are **presumed** by the court to be the **Trustee** of your Strawman's estate. The judge is acting as the **Executor** because he is the one in power who **executes** the alleged directives of the trust.

The Executor gives the orders, and the Beneficiary is **presumed** to be the State. You are **presumed** to be the **Trustee** who takes orders from the State, through the judge, and must be obedient to those orders and to the state.

The executor is the person in power - the person in charge.

The De Facto Way

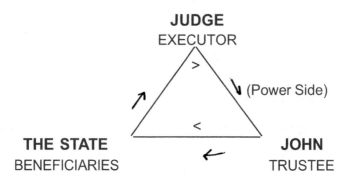

JUDGE
EXECUTOR

(Power Side)

THE STATE
BENEFICIARIES

JOHN
TRUSTEE

Power flows from the **EXECUTOR** (*JUDGE*) through the presumed **TRUSTEE** (*JOHN*) for the benefit of **THE STATE** (*the beneficiary*).

The Lawyer for the defense has not properly contracted you with the court - whether you know it or not.

Lawyers are "trained" to obey the Judge as though he were King of the Court.

Lawyers operate on the **presumption** that the Judge is the Executor and Administrator of JOHN's trust estate.

Lawyers allow the court to proceed on the false **presumption** that the Judge is the Executor and Administrator of JOHN's estate and that the State is the Beneficiary of JOHN's trust, instead of JOHN; and that JOHN is a Trustee who must take orders from the state.

As the **presumed** trustee, JOHN is liable for his lawyer's actions in the case, instead of his lawyer, himself.

His Lawyer has no commitment to JOHN. His oath is to the BAR - as the British agent of the Crown that he is.

Constitutions are irrelevant in court.

The De Jure Way

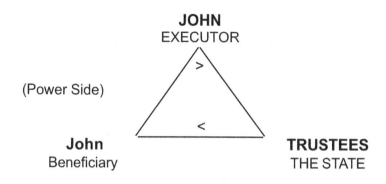

JOHN
EXECUTOR

(Power Side)

John
Beneficiary

TRUSTEES
THE STATE

Power flows from the **EXECUTOR** (*JOHN*) through his public **TRUSTEES** (*THE STATE*) for the benefit of *John* (*the beneficiary*).

His defense lawyer never tells **John** that he swore a prior oath to the Court and the British Crown.

ENFORCEMENT

The **SHERIFF** is the highest authority in his County. It is his **sworn duty** to make sure that the **State's trustees** do their Jobs as they are ordered **by their Constituents** to do.

The **SHERIFF** should hold the *Trustees (of your trust estate)* to account. If they don't do **what you order them to do**, they are in **breach of trust** because *you are the Executor* of your trust estate. **You are "The One" to execute your trust.**

Contracts make the law. Trust Law is the *highest law* there is. **Trust Law = God's Law = The Trinity.** They cannot violate Trust Law. So *rebut their presumptions* with the truth.

In Trust Law: the *Executor* hires and appoints *Trustees* to carry out his orders according to the terms of the trust for the benefit of the *Beneficiaries* of the trust.

In Corporate Law: the *Director* hires and appoints *Employees* to carry out his directions according to the Charter of the corporation for the benefit of the *Stockholders* of the corporation.

What we have forgotten (or have never been taught):

In Civil Law *We the People* (*as Executors*) elect and appoint our ***Government Officials*** (our Trustees) ***to carry out our orders*** according to the Constitutions for the united States of America and the States.

JOHN
Executor

John   TRUSTEES
Shareholder-Beneficiary   *Public trustees*

This is your three party trust estate

6

Trusts Explained

It is not difficult to understand trusts. Trusts are simply corporations in disguise. Your earthly estate is a trust. God made you the CEO (chief executive officer) of your trust estate; whether you know it or not.

Your Public power flows clockwise to your Strawman (the Executor of your trust estate) through your Public employees (the administrative trustees of your trust estate) back to you (the shareholder/beneficiary of your trust estate).

Your Government employees should be the Trustees of your trust estate, transmitting power to you — the beneficiary of your trust estate — from your Strawman.

Your Government employees are supposed to administer your trust estate according to God's plan for your benefit as the beneficiary of God's will, the New Testament Word of God, expressed in the Declaration of Independence of 1776 and the Constitution for the united States of America of 1787-91.

But the Federal government made a *"switcheroo"* (*a bait and switch*); by reversing the roles; by enticing you to accept Unilateral contracts with them; without your knowledge or consent.

A **Unilateral contract** is where party "**A**" makes a **Conditional offer** to party "**B**", to do something if "**B**" should accept the offer — where "**A**" says to "**B**" if you will do such and such, I will do this. "**A**" makes a conditional offer but asks for nothing in return except for you to meet that condition. "**A**" makes an offer seeking a **unilateral contract** with "**B**" in return.

6

"**B**" can choose to accept this offer by simply meeting the condition that is offered. "**B**" must accept the offer by performing the conditional act. No promise is asked for; only performance of the act.

At no point does "**B**" need to perform. If "**B**" chooses not to respond, and does nothing, then no contract is made. But if "**B**" meets the condition of the offer, the aggrement is confirmed and both parties are now bound by the contract terms.

When we accept a privilege or benefit offered by the Government, we *join the government* and become bound to their statutes and laws.

Each of us is unknowingly made the Trustee of a trust that the Federal government *established in our name* when we were born, *and granted to itself* — without our knowledge or consent.

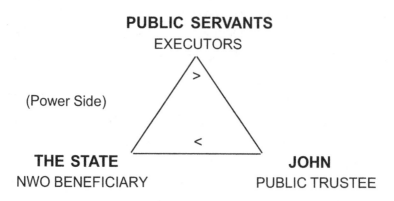

PUBLIC SERVANTS
EXECUTORS

(Power Side)

THE STATE
NWO BENEFICIARY

JOHN
PUBLIC TRUSTEE

Power flows from the *PUBLIC SERVANTS* through the presumed *PUBLIC TRUSTEE* for the benefit of the *STATE*, the *N.W.O. Beneficiary of the trust.*

As the Grantor of this trust, the Federal government made the *STATE* the Beneficiary of the trust, in your stead, and called it the *"JOHN DOE" SOCIAL SECURITY TRUST (as numbered in conjunction with your name)* which holds and manages your property in trust — for the benefit of the State instead of for you.

However, there is a way to separate from them and become free. Affirm the truth of your status and *"come out from among them and be separate."* (2 Cor. 6:17).

Rebut their presumptions and be free.

You should be The One to execute your trust.

You should be the **executor/grantor/shareholder/administrator/beneficiary** of your trust estate. Your Government servants should be the **trustees** who have to take orders from you, and be in obedience to you — the real **executor** of your trust.

In other words, the role of the **trustee** in your trust was changed from *your government servants* to *you*; and the role of the **beneficiary** in your trust was changed from *you* to *your government servants* and the *State* — for the benefit of the State — without your knowledge or consent.

The Federal government usurped your role as the **executor/administrator/director/shareholder/beneficiary** of your trust estate and made you the **trustee** of your trust estate who must take orders from the State... instead of from God.

What is the significance of this a bait and switch, you may ask? Well it is simply this:

Instead of you being the Beneficiary of your trust estate, the State made your Government servants and the State the Beneficiaries of your trust estate, instead.

As the *presumed* trustee of the public trust, you have been forced to follow the orders of the *presumed Executor* of the public trust; and to think that you are a Servant of the state, instead of them.

Until you rebut their presumptive claim.

BE THE ONE

7

Your Road To Freedom

Every phase of our lives operates in commerce. You need your strawman to operate in commerce.

Your strawman has a license to operate in commerce (i.e. drivers license, marriage license, handgun license, occupational license, building permits, etc.).

A license is good as long as you want it to be, by your permission. When there is a fine for misuse of your license, you need to learn how to then switch the strawman to the living soul with the right to life, liberty, property, and the pursuit of happiness.

The strawman is a transmitting utility that allows you to operate in commerce with a license to conduct your commercial Affairs.

Anyone operating in commerce without a license is committing a commercial crime. You and I need to learn how to become the administrator or agent for the strawman and conduct all of his/her commercial affairs without getting personally involved.

All crimes are commercial and are then regulated by commercial courts. Commercial crimes are murder, stealing, dealing in illegal drugs, prostitution, practicing law or making a legal determination without the permission or 'consent by assent' of any party to a contract.

All commerce is ruled by contracts. All courts (tribunals) are ruled by contracts. Absent a contract, the court (tribunal) will unlawfully proceed to write a contract under Cause/Case # __such and such__.

"Will the defendant rise, what is your name?" Stating your name is the signature for the contract.

"How do you plead?" Making a plea is giving the court subject matter jurisdiction which becomes part of the consideration for the contract.

All the arguments comprise the offer for the contract and the judgment initiates the acceptance of the contract; by you.

The court takes a complaint, turns it into a charge against the strawman, tries him/her on the charge and then a judgment is rendered which is a civil action, a claim, which must then be accepted by the living soul to make it valid.

Your *acceptance* makes the contract!

You accept the judgment in two ways, by your silence or by your signature when you sign the judgment; or by admitting that you "understand" (stand under) the judgment; or by appealing the judgment to a higher court (a third party) who will then agree with the judgment that you already accepted by making an appeal.

Why would you argue law or codes, rules, regulations, procedure, statutes when the contract already makes the law in your case; by your self-confession.

The Redemption Process of Acceptance for Value could otherwise then authorize the payment for the judgment. The judgment should be signed by the clerk of the court for he or she is the court.

In most cases the Judge will sign the judgment hoping that you will accept the contract by one of the first two ways, by silence or signature, or an eventual appeal to a third party.

Another response is to reject the contract under Truth in Lending within 72 hours, also, when the contract concerns mortgages, under Regulation Z and Truth in Lending.

Always remember, everything is in commerce and is ruled by contracts.

Codes, rules, regulations, procedure, and statutes apply only to the corporation that they were written for. You do not argue codes, rules, regulations, or statutes in commerce — you argue contracts. No contract, no case.

There is no contract with a policeman, government official, federal agent, or federal agency, even when you have a license.

A government or corporation is a fiction that cannot sign a contract or enforce a contract — *unless you join their corporation as an employee and argue their rules, codes, regulations, and/or procedure,* which argument they then use to enforce a contract you unwittingly made.

Commerce and Contracts — that's all there is.

BE THE ONE

8
Corporations and Contracts

My new motto is, "Know More!" (know more, and No More!) It's time to understand what's really going on, and to open our eyes and take our country back. And the best way to do this is to hit "them" where it hurts, in their financial statements!

What is the most effective way to make others change? Change *your* behavior toward *them*. If you want a child to stop being mean, you simply tell that child that until he plays "nice" you won't play with him anymore. If that child needs you, he will quickly change his ways.

So, we tell the police departments, county sheriff offices, states and the feds, that they aren't playing by the rules of full disclosure, so we won't play with them any more!

They're not cute little children. They're giant corporations that have nothing to do with lawful government. They have nothing to do with lawful government anymore, and that's the point.

America hasn't been a sovereign nation, with lawful government in more than a century. Some might argue that there never has been lawful governments, for every man is independent of all laws, except laws prescribed by nature.

"Man is not bound by any institutions formed by his fellowman without his consent." [*Cruden v. Neale,* 2 N.C. 338 (1796) 2 S.E. 70.]

The key phrase here is WITHOUT HIS CONSENT. You must voluntarily give your consent to enter into any contract with these corporations.

The "state" declares they are a "state" and this is true, but what is a "state?" The STATE OF MAINE is a sub-corporation of the UNITED STATES which is a corporation, operating in commerce for a profit, instead of for the welfare of the people.

Now some may ask, "So what, if they operate as a corporation?"

Well, if they operated as a "not for profit" corporation, and the stockholders were we the people, then that might be okay. But the fact remains that every municipality, school district, public works, state or federal agency, and the United States, is a corporation operating for profit; and you and I are NOT the stockholders.

These corporations are privately held companies that operate for a profit! Think about that for a minute. The entity we call government is actually a corporation: a foreign corporation that is not owned by the American people.

Who makes the corporations responsible to the people? Do they watch themselves and never harm anyone? No!

We have to sue XYZ Company, because they knew that their tires were causing hundreds of deaths, but XYZ Company didn't want to take responsibility because the "bottom line" was more important to them than human life.

Once the system went into corporate status, it ceased to be a government.

Prior to the system becoming a corporation, no one ever had to register to vote. Now they claim that *everyone* must be registered. This is not true. Try it sometime. Go down to vote in a local election in which you are an inhabitant of that area, but are not registered to vote. Tell them that it is your right to vote and that you don't have to be registered. Most likely you will be allowed to vote, but they may not be very friendly toward you.

You may be asking: "Doesn't 'registered' simply mean, 'signed up'?" Well, not quite.

When you "register" yourself, you "record formally and exactly ... in a list or the like."

Sounds innocent enough. Now, whom do you register with? With the Registrar. A "Registrar" is an officer who has custody of and is in charge of maintaining a registry, or register.

Some examples of registries are registries of copyrights, deeds, wills, motor vehicles, and patents. These all have to do with personal property, not people.

Other registries such as of births, deaths, marriages, voter registrations, college registrations, and the like all have to do with registering natural people. Now we are really going to take a forward leap.

What really is a "registry?" "Generally, a 'registry' applies to vessels in foreign commerce, whereas 'enrollment' refers to coastwise navigation."

When we register ourselves, we're saying that we are vessels in *foreign commerce!* Sounds ridiculous doesn't it?

This is why our names are in all upper case letters on all of the various registrations: military, voting, birth certificates, death certificates, credit cards, etc. (This essay presumes that you have an understanding of the all capitalized, fictional name vs. proper names whose first letters only are capitalized.) All vessels or ships have capitalized names.

After registering, we are no longer dealt with as natural living souls, but as *vessels operating in foreign commerce.*

What's the "foreign commerce" in which we are operating?" Corporate commerce. Corporations are *foreign to natural beings* and cannot do business with them.

We enter their jurisdiction, to do business with them, when we are viewed as vessels because we are registered as such. A vessel is a fiction, just as a corporation is a fiction. The two fictions are now capable of mutually transacting business.

This all ties in with the flag law many of us have been studying. Many people for years have said that we are now under maritime law and suggested that we study maritime/admiralty law for court.

After all, the flag flown in all of the courts is a military flag, therefore the law they are advertising by that flag is admiralty. So we are viewed as vessels because we registered as such. We are all vessels in a sea of commerce and all courts are commercial courts for commercial fictions; not lawful Common Law courts for real people.

Okay, now we are a vessel. A vessel enters contracts with other vessels under the law of the flag. If we don't like the laws their flag represents, then we should not contract with that other vessel. The flag is your warning, of what laws will have control of the contract.

When you submit a contract (which is itself a vessel), where is your flag? If your contract does not display a flag, then you are tacitly submitting to the laws of their flag. But you say there is no flag displayed on their contract. Right, and wrong. There is no flag on the face of the contract, but there is a flag somewhere in their building or in front of their building.

Every bank displays a UNITED STATES flag (not an American flag), most large corporations have the corporate UNITED STATES flag, and the corporate STATE flag and their company's own corporate flag flying in front of their buildings.

Haven't you ever wondered why big corporations have their own flags? These represent the codes, rules and regulations that govern their contracts. My neighbor's kid's college is a good example - all three flags fly right in front of the Bible building, for goodness sake! It is astounding how they disclose their intentions and we haven't a clue as to what's really going on.

Again, some one will most likely ask, "What is wrong with these flags?" Good question, BIG answer. These flags are for corporations that abide by rules, codes and regulations — NOT LAWS.

Allow me an analogy. What corporate name pops into your head when I tell you to think of a L A R G E corporation? Okay, keep that big 500-club name in mind during the following analogy.

ANALOGY:

After four grueling interviews with multiple tests, you finally land that job at the BIG Company. The boss sends you down to Human Resources to fill out paper work. One of the forms you must sign is an acknowledgment form for an Employee Handbook that states that you have received, understand, and will abide by the rules, codes and regulations of the corporation. Some of those rules will deal with dress code, tobacco usage, protocols, harassment, sick time, vacation pay and even disciplinary actions.

Excitedly, you sign the acknowledgment (contract) and start work bright and early Monday morning. You are in your finest suit with shoes polished and it's a real good hair day.

I, and your best friend, show up to take you out for a celebration lunch. I work for myself though doing landscaping and I'm in my usual attire: overalls, t-shirt and work boots.

This outfit doesn't meet the standards of the company's dress code and your coworkers look at me kind of funny, but I do NOT work for this company, nor did I agree to abide by its dress code, so they cannot tell me how to dress because they have no jurisdiction — no contract with me.

Now, you must understand that the "government" is no more than a private corporation. They have corporate codes, rules, and regulations for their corporate employees just as that big 500 Company did in our analogy. Since these codes are not laws, why does everyone follow them as if they were the law?

Why does the corporate "government" think you must follow their codes, rules and regulations? The reason is because you say that you are an employee.

You state that you are an employee of the UNITED STATES every time you file a Form 1040 with the IRS, as that form is only for government employees. So the IRS takes you at your word and treats you as an employee. The same is true for STATE taxation forms. You also assert that you are a UNITED STATES corporate employee every time you answer yes to the question, "Are you a United States citizen?"

How many times have we done that, maybe 20 or more? Think of all of the forms you have signed that ask that very question: W-4s, I-9s, passports, drivers licenses, job applications, school registrations, credit card applications, Brady Bill forms ... the list is endless.

United States (corporate) citizens are subject to all of the codes, rules and regulations of the company. If you claim national citizenship, please remember that America, or your state, is the nation to claim — NOT the UNITED STATES corporation!

Personally, this writer is an inhabitant of Maine and my citizenship is in not of this earth.

The bottom line is that when we are dealing with corporations, we are dealing with contracts [Erie Railroad vs. Thompkins].

Just as I did not have a contract with the big 500 Company and did not have to adhere to its dress code, I don't have a contract with the UNITED STATES corporation so I don't have to adhere to their employee codes.

Everything is by contract. Even the courts are corporations and operate by contract. Everything offered to you either verbally or in writing is a new 'offer of contract'.

Think, about these examples and start noticing how many times each day you get 'offers to contract': a traffic ticket; a parking ticket; a code enforcement violation for your yard not being mowed; a building permit; a jury duty notice; a notice or bill for property taxes; a bill to re-register you car; a notice or bill for state or federal taxes; a notice from your bank or credit card company that there will be higher charges for late payments; etc., the list is eternal because everything between you and a corporation is an 'offer to contract'.

The good news is that all contracts can be accepted or REJECTED.

Within a 72-hour period under the Truth in Lending Act, you can reject an 'offer to contract'. This includes rescinding contracts that you have accepted and then have for whatever reason changed your mind about accepting it.

What happens when a police officer pulls you over and gives you a ticket? Do you have a choice as to whether or not you are going to sign that ticket? Of course not!

Do you even have a choice as to how you are going to sign the ticket? No. Not anymore. My brother Syeve was stopped last week and he called me to ask how he should sign the ticket. Steve was ready when the police officer returned and handed him the ticket, but the officer told Steve to sign his name and only his name.

Wow! Forced contracts under threat, duress and coercion. Is this the land of the free, or what?

It's decision time. If we start rejecting all offers of contract that demand "money" out of our pockets, we will hit them were it hurts. Eventually they will have no choice but to shut their doors as would any business whose sales have dropped off.

The only difference between the corporate "government" and your local five and dime is that you actually get something in return for your "money" at the local five and dime.

For those of you that still believe we have to support our "government" through taxation, I simply point you to Ronald Reagan's Grace Commission Report of 1984:

100% of what is collected is absorbed solely by interest on the Federal Debt and by Federal transfer payments. In other words, all individual income tax revenues are gone before one nickel is spent on the services taxpayers expect from government.

This country operates today on the same sources of revenue as it did prior to the income tax — "duties" or "imposts" on imported goods and "excise taxes" on domestic goods that are nonessential items. This is all the revenue required to run the "government.

The next standard objection is a book in itself and requires a good deal of research to understand, but I want to try to briefly answer one more objection that most people of good moral character will raise in regard to the Federal debt. "Don't we all have to pay our debts?"

Well, if this were an honest debt, that you or I incurred and agreed to pay, then by all means the answer would be an overwhelming "YES".

However, that is not the case with the Federal debt. The Federal is the UNITED STATES corporation, again, a privately held company that artificially created this outrageous debt out of nothing, and then made you and I believe we were responsible to pay *their* debts for them.

The debt is what the corporate owners created out of nothing and lent back to their sub-corporations. It's not even a real debt — it's FRAUD (which coincidentally stands for Federal Reserve Accounting Unit Denominations).

If that big 500 corporation from our analogy came to you and said, "Hey, we need your help in getting rid of our debt," you may feel a modicum of sympathy for that corporation, but would you pay their debts for them? NO WAY.

Then why are you paying this private company's artificial and fraudulent debt, simply because they titled their corporation "UNITED STATES?"

The corporate "government" is nothing more than a pyramid scheme leaching off of the hard working productive sector today.

Back to our new motto — just say "KNOW MORE!"

Note:
All definitions are from BLACKS LAW DICTIONARY Sixth Edition.

The following accounts should help you understand the point of this essay - everything is about contracts!

Contract Story #1 as related to me in February of 2000:

"I was on my way to visit my mom in New Mexico. She just had emergency surgery and needed someone to look after her. The doctors explained that there were heart complications, so I rushed to her side. I, unfortunately, am the queen of tickets, so, now, 'rushing' to me equates to 5 miles over the posted limit. The last thing I wanted was to prolong the trip by having a police officer pull me over.

But a lesson was in the making and sure enough a Texas Highway Patrol had nothing better to do than harass me.

He badgered me into telling him why I was in a hurry, he proceeded to verify my story by calling my mother AT THE HOSPITAL! (as if she didn't have enough to worry about — she almost lost her life the day before) and then he still writes me a ticket and not for five miles over, but ten!

So I write the judge a letter explaining why **we don't have joinder** and I ask him to answer a few questions. Without knowing it, I had **rejected his offer of contract.** I don't show up by the date allowed, so the nice judge writes me a letter of extension and gives me two more weeks to appear. I call him and ask him what law he is using to prosecute the case. He doesn't even understand the question, so I say, "Is it Admiralty, Maritime, Common, Statutory, UCC, or what?"

To which he replies, "it's anything I want it to be." Well that narrows things down, doesn't it? I then ask him if this is a civil or criminal matter and he says it's both. So now I don't have a clue what law to study in order to fight this, nor do I really understand what I'm being charged under. During this phone conversation the judge tells me he isn't going to have time to go over all of this in person when I come down. I tell him that I am coming down to fight this and that he may want to have the county attorney help him look over the questions in my letter. He didn't take too kindly to that suggestion. He also said that he didn't even have a flag in his chambers, so not to worry about jurisdiction.

The day comes to appear in the judge's chambers to "talk" about the ticket". Wouldn't you know it; there is a tiny flag in the penholder on the judge's desk. Well I'll be, "No flag, huh?" There is also a county attorney that has to be present before the judge will allow my husband and I into his chambers. I begin by holding my flag, handing the judge a 4-page letter and telling, him that this is a "Special, not General, Appearance." The letter explains why the Court and I don't have joinder.

The next twenty minutes is a jurisdictional tug-o-war in which the judge and county attorney, try in earnest **to get me to plea**, including the judge telling me that he is going to enter a plea for me, to which I responded with, **"Judge, you can't practice law from the bench."**

The county attorney finally knows I'm not going to give in, so he asks, "Young lady, do you have a drivers license?" I said, "Yes sir, unfortunately I do." He then turns to the judge and says, "Judge, she has appeared before you today and she has a drivers license, so she has waived her rights." *I waived my rights???*

You know that light bulb that goes off over the heads of the cartoon characters when they get a great idea? At that very moment, that same light bulb appeared over my head. I realized that it was ALL ABOUT CONTRACTS!

Thinking quickly, I turned to the judge and asked him to remind the county attorney that **I had reserved my rights** on the face of the ticket and that I had made a **"special appearance"** *under threat of imprisonment ,* which in no way waives my rights.

The county attorney then asked the judge to grant a continuance so that he could review my 4-page letter. The judge did so and told me to return a month later. I got home and recounted the story for a friend of mine. The friend said, "Oh Ann, you just gave them jurisdiction, sit down right now and write that judge and tell him you didn't agree to that continuance." I did just that and told the judge that I wasn't coming back on that date or any other date.

This letter was a bit different. Instead of asking him to dismiss the ticket, which sounds as if I am granting jurisdiction, I demanded him to immediately **cease and desist** the proceedings under the color-of-law against the Sovereign.

Well, it has been two years and no warrants were ever issued for my arrest. Not only did I have two "insider" friends check to see if warrants were put out on me, but I was arrested (most of the best people are!!!) in December of 2001 on a contempt charge and no outstanding, warrants were on my record.

The contempt charge is what I got for trying to help a friend in court.

Don't go into their court if you can help it! I know that sometimes it's unavoidable and even necessary. You are granting jurisdiction **just by being there** if you don't know exactly how to challenge it.

Please don't play their game on their field. They have the home court advantage and the guns to back it up when they feel like it.

Contract Story #2 when I was attempting to help the same friend in story #1:

The city animal control division informed my friend that he couldn't have all of the animals he was feeding and housing. We, being the good law abiding people we are, wrote a letter to the judge inquiring as to how the city's codes could violate the Constitution.

There was no response to the letter, so after about a month, we began to inquire as to when a response would be forthcoming. As it turned out, the judge had given the letter to the city attorney and we wound up in her office discussing the matter. My friend asked questions, while I tape-recorded the conversation and one of his witnesses testified to the city attorney that animal control had actually gone into my friend's yard and taken some of the animals. The conversation eventually came to the Constitution and flag law. My friend asked what laws the city went by since we believed their codes were in direct violation of the Constitution, at which point the city attorney became visibly upset and practically yelled at my friend.

She said, "Mister Darlak, we go by the CITY OF ABILENE laws, the STATE OF TEXAS laws and the UNITED STATES laws."

As you would assume, we left that meeting in a very confused state. It took more than a year for us to understand what the city attorney had meant by her statement. She said that the city abides by CORPORATE codes. Since corporate codes are all about contract and we all have the right to contract, the city codes do not abrogate the Constitution, but she couldn't or just wouldn't disclose that to us.

That is their game, they get you to contract with them and then you're stuck, unless you know how to reject their 'offers to contract'.

Please retrain your thought processes!!!

What you and I were taught that was government is nothing more than a privately held corporation!

And what you and I were taught were laws are nothing more than **corporate codes, rules, and regulations** that have nothing to do with living souls unless you work as an employee for that company.

BE THE ONE

9
The American Dream?

March 9,1933: "A day that will go down in infamy"; spoken by Franklin Roosevelt on a different day, but applying more surely to this day too, for on this day, by the "Trading with the Enemies Act" and the declaration by Congress of the Bankruptcy of THE UNITED STATES (a corporation), the American Dream became a Nightmare instead.

Slowly but surely the Bankers proceeded to take over the Federal Court System; the taking over of which is now complete, for federal rules must now be used in state courts.

Congress — *never having lawfully assembled after Abraham Lincoln dissolved Congress when the Southern states walked out during a debate over the Civil War — nor ever having been passed into positive law* — is now seated outside of the Constitution, as the Court System is as well.

This is the reason for registering to vote, for by registering, you were given *the privilege of voting,* and any one who signs in and votes in the federal elections (or in any election) is voting as a corporate entity (a strawman) and is agreeing to the presumption that Congress has the authority to act *from its Foreign Jurisdiction.*

The entire court system is now ruled by, and under their *foreign jurisdiction flag* which has a gold fringe around the edge and a golden eagle or gold symbol above the flag, and some courts will make a mockery of the united States Flag by positioning it in a vertically gathered way, rather than set free.

The 'powers that be' knew that all commerce is ruled by the Law of contracts (better known as the UCC). No contract; no case.

The schools began to teach that any contract you signed is a valid contract that you must fulfill. This saying is true as long as the contract is between two living souls where the contract is fully disclosed to both parties and both parties agree to the terms by adding their signatures thereto. And that "Good Credit (honest credibility) is the most important thing that you have".

Well, a valid contract has five parts:

(1) Offer, (2) Acceptance, (3) Consideration, (4) Signatures of all parties to the contract, and (5) full disclosure and mutual understanding of the terms.

Only the parties that sign the contract can enforce the contract. What's more, a lawyer cannot settle any dispute that may arise from a contract without both parties' consent.

The Creator created Man with the unalienable right to govern himself and to form a government. Man gave government the right to form corporations.

As man has no right to rule his Creator, God; a government has no right to rule its creator, Man. A government can only govern what it creates. Government created a legal fiction to rule by giving it a corporate name and assuming man to be that a legal fiction and writing his name in all CAPITAL LETTERS with the middle NAME only an initial, or not at all.

The proper name for a living soul is written in upper and lower case letters, the first and middle name being the Sovereign name and the last name being the family name. The real name for a living soul is I, Me, My, or Myself.

Government is only a piece of paper, being a creation of mankind. As the government, being a piece of paper, could only create a CORPORATION, which in itself is not able to sign a lawful contract with a living soul.

All CORPORATIONS must have someone to speak for them, and the government came up with a solution, the Lawyer, who has been appointed to speak for all Corporations in the Courts which they have created.

The government then devised an alternate to the Lawful Contract called the "Unilateral Contract", or one-signature contract.

Their own description of the unilateral contract says that they were probably written up by a lawyer or a group of lawyers to commit fraud with the intent to extort monies from the signers. The lawful problem with these contracts (aside from the fact that they only have the signature of one party to the contract) is that they have many hidden traps about which the party is unaware.

In many cases such as bank contracts or signatures for checking purposes, the contract is never shown to the depositor. All contracts pertaining to Corporations signed by a one party participant are fraud from their conception and are used to extort monies from the people.

They cannot be enforced except with our permission or 'consent by assent'.

From the beginning, men have the right to Contract with whomever or for whatever they so choose. The government then set their court system apart from the Constitution and its people and then invites the people to Contract with their Court system under their Foreign Jurisdiction Flag, to allow them to settle their disputes.

Since a "person " is to the government as a CORPORATION, they treat any living soul, who contracts with their Court, as a CORPORATION as well, and as a "Legal Person " and a slave ordebtor which cannot speak for itself.

The first thought that enters the minds of people when they receive a letter from a lawyer saying "You have been sued" is to hire another lawyer to settle the dispute between the two corporations in their corporate court. The Judge protects the lawyers, and they in turn protect the court; for they are officers of the court.

The system is call a "legal system"; meaning that what they are doing is legal; legal simply meaning **with your consent.**

After they gain your consent, the system then becomes lawful **with your consent** for whatever they choose to do to you.

Law or lawfulness is constitutional in subject matter for no law can be enacted (or is supposed to be) without an **enabling clause** from the constitution of the state or for the united States of America.

The court does not have a contract with a party until the party gives the judge his or her name; until that time the judge is simply an actor in a black robe. Until then, the court is trying to get the party to contract with it under their Foreign Jurisdiction Flag.

Since judges do not file their oath of office into their courtroom, they act under administrative law as however they may choose.

The Laws passed since 1926 have all been signed by the president of the BAR (the British Accredited Regency) of the state of New York, bringing all laws under the BAR as nothing more that BAR codes, rules, regulations, statutes, and procedures for the corporations to follow.

The only way you have to make the judge uphold his oath is to file his oath into the case and restrict him to the type of law that **you** want to follow.

There are seven *Demands for Discovery* to demand of all lawyers:

(1) Produce the legislative act and its implementing regulations that precipitated this cause;

(2) Produce the legislative act that created the office of lawyer, attorney, counselor, esquire; give me the address of his office where I may go and get a license to practice law;

(3) Produce a copy of your oath of office as an officer of the court and where you filed it into the public record;

(4) Produce the contract signed by Myself, proper name of the living soul, and You (name of the lawyer), in which I agreed to give up my constitutional rights.

(5) Give Me your name, address, and phone number.

(6) Give Me your bond number and your bonding company name, address, and location.

(7) Send me an acknowledgment that you understand that you have perjured your oath of office and are committing Constructive Treason against the Constitution for the united States of America, the State of Maine and the American Peace Flag.

Under this system of consent, a living soul never has to accept the ruling of the court — but they must object at all times to the action being taken. All persons spending time in prison were sent there by their own words.

Example: Judge: "Did you receive a fair trial?" Answer. "Yes" (The party is just being railroaded). "Did your lawyer fight hard for you?" Answer "Yes". "Do you feel that 12 years is a reasonable sentence?" Answer "Yes". You just sentenced *yourself* to prison.

This is aided and abetted by the parties' lawyer who has

just told him to be nice to the judge in the sentence phase of his "trial" and tells the party that the judge is probably going to give him a 12 year sentence instead of the 50 year sentence he could get.

The other part of the problem is with the laws in today's court — or the total lack of laws. The charge and intent are combined in one charge so you cannot plead innocent — you must plead guilty, not guilty, or no contest — thereby giving the court jurisdiction over the case.

All the courts have been lumped together into one court Administrative/Admiralty/Civil (contract/commerce).

With the kaking of your plea, you go administratively under any law they want to use to convict you.

In order for a law to be construed as law it must have an enacting clause from the source the law came from, i.e. King, legislature, etc. All laws proceeding from the state legislatures must have an enacting clause; "Be it enacted by the Legislature of the State of Maine..."

A legislature can only introduce a bill; it cannot introduce a law. The bill must go through, be approved unanimously by the House, signed by the Leader of the House, be approved by the Senate, signed by the Leader of the Senate, approved and signed by the Governor, and then the bill becomes Law.

Now it is checked against the Constitution to find the enabling clause from which it was written. If the Constitution does not allow for the law, then it is void from it inception.

Have you ever heard that a party can challenge the Enacting part of the law or the Subject Matter Jurisdiction of the matter he or she is being tried for violating at any time of the trial or even upon conviction, while in prison? Usually it is not a law that a party is being tried for breaking, but a code, rule, or regulation, or breach of contract.

The proper response to "You have been sued" is the Redemption Process, or Rejection, returning their contract unsigned within three days in full accord with Truth In Lending. Never let an Attorney or Lawyer send you any document without "Accepting it for Value" or "Rejecting and Returning it without Signature" in three days in full accord with Truth In Lending.

They may say anything to you in their first letter and you may think it is harmless. A Rattlesnake seems harmless and makes a pretty noise, but is deadly when it strikes.

Have you ever heard the phrase "You don't need to respond"? Do not believe it. Respond with the Redemption process or "Reject and Return it without Signature" in three days in full accord with Truth In Lending.

DON'T CONTRACT WITH THIRD PARTIES — tell them to get lost. Tell them that they are Fired!

We now understand that the government gains Power of Attorney over us when we are born and they take our birth certificates and make negotiable instruments out of them. We now know that through the Social Security Administration and the issuance of the SSNumber, we are recorded as a "TRUST" and the living soul is made the "TRUSTEE" instead of the EXECUTOR that you should be of the "STRAWMAN TRUST" that they created.

We now have our own POWER OF ATTORNEY IN FACT and we now know which form to fill out for taxes.

ALREADY WE HAVE WON!

BE THE ONE

10

Redemption Timeline

There have been so many papers written about the Redemption Process and yet there seems to be a lack of understanding of the basic concepts.

Redemption is the initial path taken by people who know they are free but see no hope in the judicial system as it is practiced today.

It is vitally important to understand how the people in the government turned our lives upside down and have made us believe that WE are subject to THEM; when in reality THEY are subject to US — every being is part and partial of We The People.

Key points:

1. In 1871, the Federal Government formed itself into a CORPORATION and pulled itself out from under the Constitution.

2. In 1913, the Federal Reserve Central Banks were created.

3. In 1933, President Roosevelt rewrote and reinstituted "Trading with the Enemies Act" of 1917. This applies only to 14th Amendment Citizens of the federal UNITED STATES.

4. In 1933, President Roosevelt took the gold away from the People — although they were not required to give it away — thereby leaving the people without "Money" for paying their "DEBTS".

5. In 1933, President Roosevelt passed HJR 192 of June 5, 1933 — simply put — since the government had taken the gold, and the people had no "Money" — the government would pay the "DEBTS" for the people — DOLLAR FOR DOLLAR — thereby giving the people-unlimited Credit.

6. In 1938, *Erie Railroad vs. Thompkins* made Contracts the rule of law in our Courts.

7. In 1946, we lost our government and courts through the Administrative Procedures Act.

8. In 1965, silver was taken away as a means for paying "DEBT", the UCC became the supreme law for America concerning the Banking System, and the courts were pulled together in Administrative/Admiral/Civil (contract or commerce/corporation), and the Act and Intent were brought together thereby taking away any plea of Innocent. You have to now prove there was no Intent. Guilty until proven innocent; changing the often quoted phrase, "You are innocent until proven guilty."

11
General Instructions

Some of this information is simply personal opinion and preference, so please study the issues and make up your own mind about everything you choose to do.

1. Answer immediately your correspondence. Do not put your paper work off.

2. Never answer a third party; respond with a rejection of contract offer — **"I reject your offer of contract"** — telling him and all of his heirs, agents and assigns that they are third parties and to get out of your commercial affairs.

3. Always send the rejected offers of contract back to the entity that sent them to you ("return to sender") and then copy anyone else involved, i.e. If you get a summons/complaint taped to your front door and it doesn't say where it came from – it probably came from the Sheriff. Reject it and send it back to the Sheriff via certified or registered mail. Then copy the court and the other party to the summons (usually a lawyer). If you get it in the mail, make sure you look at the return address because sometimes a service company sends it to you. It must be rejected and sent back to the service company ("return to sender") and then all other parties copied on it.

4. Always remember they are after subject matter jurisdiction.

5. The only thing involved in any controversy or court case is about jurisdiction.

6. Subject Matter Jurisdiction (SMJ) is the same as challenging the court's jurisdiction, but in a nicer way. Instead of

telling the judge that the court doesn't have jurisdiction over you, you are telling the court that they don't have jurisdiction over the subject matter to hear the case. This gives them an out. SMJ is over **you the living person** and that is why they never have it. They must have first hand knowledge and be a party to your contract, but they never do nor are. Don't argue the charge, the amount, or anything other that SMJ because when you start to argue the issues, you grant SMJ. (Maxim, "arguments are for fools.")

7. Subject matter jurisdiction can only be gained with your permission by 'consent or assent'. Warning: making a plea grants consent!

8. Everything they do against us in court is by affidavit and usually without any notice to us. You must check the court file daily to see if any one has placed an affidavit against you and you must **rebut every affidavit with an affidavit point by point.** We will be lawful though, and give grace and notice with our affidavits. So if you rebut an affidavit or generate an affidavit, always send it to the person it is against (copy the court clerk if it is involving a court case) giving them personal notice and a grace period to rebut it. You must include a rebuttal address for them to send a re-buttal to. Either your address or a notary's address. I suspect that the notary is the one who should receive the rebuttal.

9. What we are finding out is that even though we do an affidavit into court challenging subject matter jurisdiction, that unless you go in to the court at the appointed court time and stand up for the affidavit, the judge will put a default judgment against you. We have added a cease and desist order to our affidavits, which may take care of having to go into court, but this has not yet been establish. Some stu-

dents will not use the zip code as it is for federal jurisdictions only, creates jurisdiction, and sets up a pattern that you are a federal citizen. Sample address is as follows:

Jack Rabbit Patriot, Non-domestic
c/o 123 Bayview Drive
Portland, Maine [04105] (zip code in brackets OK)

10. Also, only use a stamp because that doesn't create a jurisdictional problem, but their stamp machines may.

11. You can take jurisdiction of all letters you send, return receipt request cards, envelopes, etc. by signing your autograph in red ink at the bottom right on both the front and the back sides of the pages/cards/ envelopes etc. and make sure you write it where no one else can sneak a number or a mark past it to the right or underneath your autograph.

12. "With the Autograph" is used instead of "Signature" under the living man's name because a signature is only the sign of someone's name/authority. It is not their real name. Do you ever hear anyone chasing a movie star or famous sports hero saying: "Hey, give me your signature." No, it's always, "Can I have your autograph?"

13. "With the Copy-Claim" is used because anything you copyright/copy-claim is protected from being used against you in a court of law unless you introduce it as evidence yourself. Please read through your documents carefully to ensure that all names/addresses or other information has been written correctly and to ensure that you know clearly what you are sending out. You are responsible for your documents – no one else.

14. In a Negative Averment, list your town and any town of anyone who is coming against you. For instance if a judge in another town is sending you a summons, then list his town

and state too.

15. In a Negative Averment, it might be wise to hand write the following statement in red ink: *"I am not a fictional limited entity! I am a natural born child of the Creator, YHWH.   I am not a surety or accommodation party for any fictitious person."* Some people choose to use the Creator's Hebrew name that He tells Moses to tell the Israelites because they believe it carries the weight of truth. Obviously this will be a personal religious conviction.

16. Any and all of this information can be changed to suit your particular beliefs of situation. This is your information, not mine, so do as you see fit, just include that *"I am not a fictional limited liability entity otherwise known as a corporation."*

12
Proverbs of Law

1. You cannot be bound to a contract if you were hood-winked.

2. It is impossible for you to be in a contract with the government, but no fraud exists when you're not contesting your rights.

3. "Produce your proof of claim for what you're alleging that I cannot do; other than doing harm."

4. Your rights have a price attached to them. You might send a fee schedule and notice that any of your rights is worth $1 million dollars, non negotiable.

5. My offers are non negotiable.

6. Think of your domain as a car lot where your office (person) is located, and your rights, as the cars sitting there for sale, with advance notice that violating any of your rights is worth $1 million dollars. Whether they buy, or not, is their choice. These are your rules; for your domain.

7. "It's your choice to violate my rights."

8. It's my jurisdiction; it's my domain; as long as I do no harm.

9. Send me evidence of what I cannot do, as long as I do no harm.

10. I am the executor and beneficiary of my estate; and I'm telling the trustees what my rights are worth.

11. Assuming liability: He who assumes the liability is in the seat of power because he is the one who is liable. He's the one who dictates orders to his trustees. He's assuming

the risk; they are a limited liability corporation.

12. When you go into their game with full liability they never can win. They're limited liability and you are not.

13. "Yes, I am that name; I accept full liability."

14. It's not about your name; it's about who you are in their game. What position are you playing in their game? What role are you playing?

15. If you're Man, you're the executor and beneficiary of your estate.

16. A trust has been created in your name; via a trust agreement under trust law.

17. A hearing is being conducted for a legal person in whom you have an interest.

18. Think of the corporate structure of a trust. There are three parties to a trust. The **director** [or board of directors]; the **employees** [the trustees] who perform the functions of government; and the **shareholders** [the beneficiaries] who appoint and control the directors.

19. The shareholders can remove the directors, because equity is king.

20. A corporation is a trust agreement, therefore the UNITED STATES, INC. is a corporate, trust.

21. My parents invested my abilities in the corporate UNITED STATES, making me a beneficiary of the trust.

22. Any time I perform a function of government I'm acting as a government employee; a government trustee who takes orders from the state.

23. I own all the equity in the trust; all the **credit** in the corporate UNITED STATES.

24. I am the director who directs the trustees of the trust; and who appoints and directs the congress of the corporate UNITED STATES.

25. I own all the equity in the trust. I am the director of the trust. I set the policy of the trust.

26. Their statutes have no effect on my beneficiary; my legal person strawman.

27. It's my job to protect my investment in the trust; my investment in the corporate UNITED STATES.

28. All I need to do is state my position in the game. I can confirm my position in the corporate UNITED STATES.

29. I am a **grantor/shareholder/beneficiary** of the corporate UNITED STATES TRUST. I can appoint the board of directors of the trust who set the policy of the trust and who ate to direct the actions of its trustees *for my benefit* according to the Constitution for the United States of America and the Bill of Rights.

30. Are you challenging my claim that I am the director of the legal person?

31. My signature created the corporation.

32. It's a trust agreement between us and the government that made it an entity.

33. I put everything into the trust. I don't remember at that point signing anything that I was going to obey government statutes, so nothing outside applies to my corporation.

34. I'"m here regarding the matter for my legal person. My name is President and CEO for that corporation."

35. Establish your title at the head of the documents you write; or at the beginning of the trial.

36. Your name is your title; in other words: Your title is your name.

37. I am the chairman of my board, and only I call board meetings.

38. I am the sole shareholder of my trust who appointed me as the director of my estate.

39. The matter before the court is the hearing for the legal person. "I am the **president/director/administrator/ agent** for that legal person. Which one do you want me to be?"

40. Courtrooms are platforms for government employees.

41. You're establishing your authority on the record with that court.

42. All you have to be is the sole beneficiary to be fully in control and appoint the director.

43. The sole shareholder is the beneficiary who appoints the administrator who directs the public employees to act according to the constitution (the charter) of the trust.

44. Statutes apply only to public employees.

45. If you're not performing a function of government they can't enforce an income tax upon you; the income tax Title 26 only applies to government employees.

46. You're supposed to perform a duty, and they're supposed to perform a duty, or else mutual consideration does not exist.

47. "If you don't agree with me, you have 21 days to respond with proof of claim to the contrary."

48. Are you claiming that I am an employee required to obey the statutes of the UNITED STATES?

49. Is there something you're claiming I can't do; other than create harm?

50. He's going to the penalty box because he broke one of the rules of the game when he was playing hockey.

51. If you agree to be an employee you must abide the employee rules, for if you don't you get punished.

52. You want to give notice to the government first thing.

53. If you have a business relationship with government,

establish your role at the outset to avoid presumptions.

54. The Birth Certificate is proof that I am a shareholder in the corporate UNITED STATES; it's the receipt for my trust foundation investment. ***Shareholders receive dividends.***

55. I own all the equity in that thing (in JOHN DOE).

56. If you're disputing that fact, feel free to let me know; arguments are for fools.

57. Shareholders appoint directors, and can remove them for good cause.

58. Clarify the game before problems arise; send notice from JOHN DOE as **director/administrator**.

59. Who am I? ... I am **man/director/administrator**.

60. Are you looking for the legal person?

61. Presumptions are not facts until both parties agree.

62. Send notice of default; then a certificate of default. You're the director in charge.

63. "The legal person has been charged with such and such by the plaintiff — OVERRULED", signed, Director.

64. Establish who you are beforehand.

65. The Birth Certificate is the true seat of power; it's proof of your/m shareholder investment in the corporate UNITED STATES.

66. File that proof in the court record.

67. The court is the boardroom of the corporate UNITED STATES.

68. It's not a fact until both parties agree.

69. If the judge issues an order as an employee of the state, who can overrule him? Yes. The director in charge!

70." The legal person has been charged with such and such — Overruled", signed, Director.

71. There's no injured party in a statutory offense.

72. "I'm the director of my legal person."

73. The corporation has asked for this amount of money. Good, tell them to pay it. — It's over at this point.

74. Preemptively contract them and establish the rules.

75. The court is the upper management of the trustees.

76. You're on the board of directors of the corporate UNITED STATES. Claim your title; establish who you are.

77. Let them know who you are before you appear. You can't establish your identity without letting them know who you are.

78. Establish the power structure, in mind and in court.

79. Contact the government's attorney general and assert your rights; and stop driving with a license plate at all.

80. They need your/my tax exemption.

81. Put a plate on, that has some identifying marks, so when they run the plate they know that it is you, and you're not to be mortgaged.

82. Notice them with a fee schedule. If you see the number and you pull me over it costs this much.

83. "You have no reason to pull me over. **I'm not performing a function of government;** I'm not a government agent or employee."

84. No one owns title to the legal person.

85. My parents gifted my abilities to the U.S. Corporate Trust.

86. John Doe is the **grantor/shareholder/beneficiary** of his trust.

87. JOHN DOE is the **executor/administrator** of his trust.

88. Gov't employees are the **administrative trustees** of my trust.

89. Corporate law mirrors trust law.

90. Shareholders appoint directors; directors set policy; directors tell the employees what to do; directors give orders to the employees, which they must obey to avoid breach of trust.

91. Employees carry out the director's orders.

92. I'm a shareholder in the corporate UNITED STATES TRUST. *Shareholders receive dividends.*

93. Trust Law = Corporate Law = the Holy Trinity

94. The owner of the equity controls.

95. Appoint yourself as the director; only two roles left, government and government employees.

96. Everybody is an agent for the legal person according to the role he plays.

97. The Constitution only applies to the government.

98. Statutes and regulations only apply to government residents and employees.

99. My Birth Certificate has the government's signature on it; therefore the government owes an obligation to me. *Shareholders receive dividends.*

100. Applications for benefits create public servants with titles.

101. Public servants are taxpayers who owe taxes.

102. Complaints are made against public servants.

102. SSN's are optional for non interest bearing accounts.

103. Statutes and regulations only apply to government employees.

102. If I'm assuming liability for the actions of someone else I have a right to control what he does.

103. If you're assuming full liability for your actions, and you never intentionally cause harm, you can never be held accountable for what you might accidentally do.

104. Unintentionally causing harm is not causing harm according to law, because it was not intentional; it just happened, so you're not actually liable. Intent is everything in law.

105. They never reply to affidavits because it would be perjury on their part. They can't prove anything. They never try to prove anything.

106. You have to enter a plea in their jurisdiction for a hearing to proceed.

107. Any ID from the government is not good because it identifies you as having applied for a benefit making you a public servant where the government assumes all liability for your actions and therefore has the right to control you.

108. It's not their responsibility to teach you who you are.

109. Remove presumptions; establish the terms.

110. You never have to make a plea.

111. There's no reason to go to court, until you win.

112. Send it in to the courthouse in writing with a motion to dismiss, long before you have to show up before the court. Let them know you're not going to come, write, "I believe that default judgment is for public servants and I haven't seen any evidence that proves that I am a public servant."

113. "I have not seen any facts nor have I been provided with any evidence that I am a public servant and I believe that no such evidence exists." Send this in to the court with a motion to dismiss.

114. You are not compelled to enter a plea.

115. A trial cannot commence until a plea has been made. No plea; No trial.

116. "I don't allow you to enter a plea for me; you can't legislate from the bench. I will not enter a plea until I see a claim made against me; everything else is irrelevant."

117. Default Judgment is not a court of record.

118. Transcripts are not a matter of public record; file transcripts in the court record, anything of record is in common law jurisdiction.

119. Get a certified copy of what you submit to the court, in return.

120. If it's boxed off, it's not part of the document.

121. The court can't hear a jurisdictional challenge; no one (judge) can rule on his own cause.

122. Make your case a court of record by swearing out an affidavit and filing it with the court, then it's up to the state to rebut it point by point.

123. Who brought the complaint to the court? ... The state.

124. The state said we're disobeying orders, so we address the state first, before time for court.

125. "Prove that I was acting as an agent of government at the time of the complaint."

126. Just because you showed a driver's license doesn't prove you were acting in that capacity at that time.

127. I can make a statement about what I was doing at the time. This I can prove; all else is presumption.

128. They're a private corporation.

129. Never talk with them without being charged. You have a right to remain silent. Anything you may say can be used against you in a court of law. (the Miranda note).

130. If it is not a matter of public record it never happened.

131. "I'm here regarding that matter and I'm convening a court of record."

132. Deal with the state before you go into a hearing.

133. This document is a matter of public record (header of document).

134. "Are you claiming that I was a public servant when the complaint was made?"

135. Produce the payroll record to show that I was a public servant performing a function of government.

136. DO NO HARM! ... All else is OK.

137. Government statutes apply only to government agents.

138. Unless you're a government servant, you can't be charged with a statutory offense.

139. My Birth Certificate makes me the director of my legal person estate.

140. Only man can create value.

141. Corporate law is trust law as well.

142. Equity in commerce is king.

143. "I don't believe that I am a public servant and haven't been shown any evidence supporting that presumption, and I believe that no such evidence exists."

144. Send it into the court. File it with a motion to dismiss the charge.

145. Never go to court unless you've won, and only for default judgment.

146. "If no timely rebuttal is received, it is agreed that you agree with me."

147. It is my belief that I own by property in "fee simple" as defined in Black's Law dictionary not as "joint tenant in common".

148. Your act does not apply to me.

149. Facts are agreements of the parties.

150. Government is not my enemy unless they try to force something upon me.

151. Establish a fee schedule.

152. We are all Peace officers.

153. Identify yourself *your* way.

154. No plate = no jurisdiction to tow.

155. Don't use statutes to defend yourself.

156. Watch the meaning of the words you use; i.e., aboriginal=unclean=abnormal; original-clean-normal; Citizenship = on the Citizen's ship.

157. Seldom verbally state your name: write it down; or spell it out instead.

158. Is there something you're claiming I can't do; other than not cause harm?

159. Write a default certificate and file it into the record.

160. Remove the presumptions at the start.

161. It's impossible for anyone else to assume liability for you.

162. Don't play the word definition game.

163. You're in the private domain.

164. Traffic = commerce = jurisdiction = performing a function of government

165. "I was not performing a function of government at the time, although I have a license to do so if I wish."

166. They're my roads; not the government's roads.

167. I am the public.

168. The government only has jurisdiction over commercial performers when performing a function of government.

169. "I have a license, but I am not on duty in that regard."

170. You applied for that license, to perform a function of government.

171. Give notice. Give notice. Give notice. Nobody likes to be surprised.

172. "My plate is evidence of a fee schedule in place."

173. I'm going to be accessing the public roads with my flag on my vessel.

174. The Trespass Act: Re: private property = my body = my rights.

175. Contract with the DOT.

176. Tag text: "DR DOT ME" "Not for Hire" "Private Property."

177. Give 10 days notice; 3 days to think it over, plus 3 days to deny, plus 3 days for the mail, plus 1 day of grace = 10 days.

178. Default, then send notice of default, then file copies in the court.

179. Don't go to court unless you have already won.

180. $1 million dollars is not excessive damages for an accidental death charge.

181. We extend the privilege of using the public roads to the foreign corporation to operate on our soil.

182. To the public servant officer: "Did you observe me breaching the peace? Are you claiming that I am a public servant?"

183. "I'm sorry but I don't have any ID showing that I am an agent of the government.

184. Am I under arrest? Am I free to go? Do you have a warrant for my arrest? Arrest me or let me go."

185. "I don't know who you are without knowing your badge number and name."

186. Freedom - Responsibility

187. He who does not deny admits.

188. Government is merchant's law.

189. The contract makes the law between parties.

190. In a Republic, citizens elect officers to manage public servants for the benefit of the citizens.

191. In a Corporation, shareholders elect directors to direct employees for the benefit of corporate shareholders.

192. In a Trust, grantors appoint executors to manage trustees for the benefit of the grantors.

193. In the Court, the corporation appoints judges to sustain or dismiss charges against the accused for the benefit of the state.

BE THE ONE

THE TEN MAXIMS OF COMMERCIAL LAW

10 MAXIMS OF LAW

1. *Exodus 20:15; Lev. 19:13; Mat. 10:10; Luke 10:7; II Tim. 2:6.*

2. *God's Law; Natural and Moral law; Exodus 21:23-25; Lev. 24: 17-21; Deut. 1:17, 19:21; Mat. 22:36-40; Luke 10:17; Col. 3:25.*

3. *Exodus 20:16; Ps. 117:2; John 8:32; II Cor. 13:8.*

4. *Lev. 5:4-5; Lev. 6:3-5; Lev. 19:11-13: Num. 30:2; Mat. 5:33; James 5:12.*

5. *1 Pet. 1:25; Heb. 6:13-15.*

6. *Heb. 6:16-17.*

7. *Heb. 4:16; Phil. 4:6; Eph. 6:19-21.*

8. *Book of Job; Mat. 10:22.*

9. *No willingness to sacrifice = no liability, responsibility, authority or measure of conviction; "nothing ventured nothing gained."*

10. *Gen. 2-3; Matthew 4; Revelation.*

10 MAXIMS OF LAW

1. A workman is worthy of his hire.
2. All men are equal under the law.
3. In commerce truth is sovereign.
4. Truth is expressed in the form of an affidavit.
5. An unrebutted affidavit stands as truth in commerce.
6. An unrebutted affidavit becomes judgement in commerce.
7. A matter must be expressed to be resolved.
8. He who leaves the field of battle first loses by default.
9. Sacrifice is the measure of credibility
10. A lien or claim can be satisfied only through rebuttal by counter affidavit point by point, resolution by jury, or payment or performance of the claim.

BE THE ONE

13
Other Maxims of Law

When Jesus spoke the Truth to his accusers, he would justify himself by quoting the **Law**. First, he would quote God's Law, and after quoting God's Law He would often quote the accuser's law and use that against them as well. For example, Jesus would say, "Did ye never read in the **scriptures**..." and then **quote God's Law**.

Then he would turn around and say, "Is it not written in **your law**..." and **quote their own law!** His accusers would have no answer, they could not overcome Him. How could anyone overcome somebody who is obeying both God's Law and man's law!? **If a man made law is just it will be in harmony with God's Law, the basis of common law.**

This is the purpose of this chapter. These maxims are the foundation and principles of the laws that man passes today. Unfortunately, men enforce their own will more than they enforce law. So, this is why, in addition to knowing God's Law, it is also important to know man's law as well, because man's law is based upon God's Law. And when you are accused of "breaking the law," you can do what Jesus did, and use both God's Law and man's law to justify your lawful acts, for this is the only thing that will excuse you.

Maxims of law are not commercial law but are mostly based upon scripture and truth.

Here is a court case which demonstrates a typical example of the fruitlessness of describing oneself in the terms of the world, as distinguished from whom and what our Heavenly Father has told us we are.

It was rendered by JOHN V. PARKER, Chief Judge:

"Petitioner's shield of the "Common Law" as an **"Unenfranchised Sovereign Individual of the United States of America, a Republic,"** provides him with the same degree of protection from federal income taxation as did the Ghost Dance of the Sioux warrior from the repeating rifles of the federal Calvary - ZERO protection." *(599 F.Supp. 126, George E. McKinney, Sr. v. Donald Regan, Secretary of the Treasury, et al., Civ. A. No. 84-470-A., United States District Court, M.D. Louisiana, November 19, 1984).*

But note: The *real issue* here is not *who* the Petitioner is but *where* he is. The *real issue* here is a matter of *jurisdiction.* The Petitioner must make a distinction between **the territorial United States** and **the for profit UNITED STATES CORPORATION**.

Many insist on using the "common law" to defend themselves. The reason we should not is because, first and foremost, you do not see the term "common law" in scripture. **Bondservants of Christ** are only to use God's Law. Secondly, the common law is a commercial law today, created by merchants, influenced by Roman Law, and used for commercial purposes. The following definitions are taken from "*A Dictionary of Law, by William C. Anderson, 1893.*"

Custom of merchants: A system of customs, originating among merchants, and allowed for the benefit of trade as part of the <u>common law</u>. *Page 303.*

Law-merchant; law of merchants: The rules applicable to commercial paper were <u>transplanted into the common law</u> from the law merchant. They had their origin in the customs and course of business of merchants and bankers, and are now recognized by the courts because they are demanded by <u>the wants and conveniences</u> of the mercantile world. *Pages 670-671.*

Roman Law: The <u>common law</u> of England has been largely influenced by the Roman law, in several respects:...Through the development of <u>commercial law</u>. *Page 910.*

All of man's laws, except for many maxims of law, are commercial in nature.

The following are the definitions of "maxims," and then the relevant maxims of law will be listed.

Maxim (*Bouvier's Law Dictionary, 1856*): An established principle or proposition. A principle of law universally admitted, as being just and consonant with reason.

2. Maxims in law are somewhat like axioms in geometry. *(1 Bl. Com. 68)*. They are principles and authorities, and part of the general customs or common law of the land; and are of the same strength as acts of parliament, when the judges have determined what is a maxim; which belongs to the judges and not the jury. *(Terms do Ley; Doct. & Stud. Dial. 1, c. 8)*. Maxims of the law are holden for law, and all other cases that may be applied to them shall be taken for granted. *(1 Inst. 11. 67; 4 Rep. See 1 Com. c. 68; Plowd. 27, b)*.

3. The application of the maxim to the case before the court, is generally the only difficulty. The true method of making the application is to ascertain how the maxim arose, and to consider whether the case to which it is applied is of the same character, or whether it is an exception to an apparently general rule.

4. The alterations of any of the maxims of the common law are dangerous. *(2 Inst. 210)*.

Maxim (William C. Anderson's *A Dictionary of Law, (1893), page 666):* So called...because it's value is the highest and its authority the most reliable, and because it is accepted by all persons at the very highest.

2. The principles and axioms of law, which are general propositions flowing from abstracted reason, and not accommodated to times or men, are wisely deposited in the breasts of the judges to be applied to such facts as come properly before them.

3. When a principle has been so long practiced and so universally acknowledged as to become a maxim, it is obligatory as part of the law.

Maxim of Law (*Black's Law Dictionary,* 3rd Edition, *(1933), page 1171*): An established principle of proposition. A principle of law universally admitted as being a correct statement of the law, or as agreeable to reason. Coke defines a maxim to be "a conclusion of reason" *(Coke on Littleton, 11a)*. He says in another place, "A maxim is a proposition to be of all men confessed and granted without proof, argument, or discourse." *(Coke on Littleton. 67a).*

Maxim (*Black's Law Dictionary,* 4th Edition): Maxims are but attempted general statements of rules of law and are law only to the extent of application in adjudicated cases."

These maxims are taken directly from man's law dictionaries and court cases. The following books were referenced for this chapter:

Bouvier's Law Dictionary, *by John Bouvier, (1856)*

Legal Maxims, *by Broom and Bouvier, (1856)*

A Dictionary of Law, *by William C. Anderson, (1893)*

Black's Law Dictionary, *by Henry Campell Black, (3rd, 4th, 5th, and 6th Editions, 1933-1990)*

Accidents and Injury

• An act of God does wrong to no one.

• The act of God does no injury; that is, no one is responsible for inevitable accidents.

• No one is held to answer for the effects of a superior force, or of an accident, unless his own fault has contributed.

• **The execution of law does no injury.**

• An action is not given to one who is not injured.

• An action is not given to him who has received no damages.

• He who suffers a damage by his own fault, has no right to complain.

• Mistakes, neglect, or misconducts are not to be regarded as accidents.

• Whoever pays by mistake what he does not owe, may recover it back; but he who pays, knowing he owes nothing; is presumed to give.

• **What one has paid knowing it not to be due, with the intention of recovering it back, he cannot recover back.**

• No man ought to be burdened in consequence of another's act.

• There may be damage or injury inflicted without any act of injustice.

• Not every loss produces and injury.

• A personal injury does not receive satisfaction from a future course of proceeding.

• Wrong is wiped out by reconciliation.

• An injury is extinguished by the forgiveness or reconcilement of the party injured. [Luke 17:3-4, 2 Corinthians 2:7-8]

Benefits and Privileges

• Favors from government often carry with them an enhanced measure of regulation.

• **Any one may renounce a law introduced for his own benefit.**

• No one is obliged to accept a benefit against his consent.

• He who receives the benefit should also bear the disadvantage.

• **He who derives a benefit from a thing, ought to feel the disadvantages attending it.**

• He who enjoys the benefit, ought also to bear the burden.

• He who enjoys the advantage of a right takes the accompanying disadvantage.

• **A privilege is, as it were, a private law.**

• A privilege is a personal benefit and dies with the person.

• One who avails himself of the benefits conferred by statute cannot deny its validity.

• **What I approve I do not reject. I cannot approve and reject at the same time. I cannot take the benefit of an instrument, and at the same time repudiate it.**

• He who does any benefit to another for me is considered as doing it to me.

Commerce

• *Caveat emptor* (let the buyer beware).

• Let the purchaser beware.

• Let the seller beware.

• The payment of the price stands in the place of a sale.

• **The payment of the price of a thing is held as a purchase.**

• Goods are worth as much as they can be sold for.

• Mere recommendation of an article does not bind the vendor of it.

• It is settled that there is to be considered the home of each one of us where he may have his habitation and account-books, and where he has made an establishment of his business.

• No rule of law protects a buyer who willfully closes his ears to information, or refuses to make inquiry when circumstances of grave suspicion imperatively demand it.

• Let every one employ himself in what he knows.

• He at whose risk a thing is done, should receive the profits arising from it.

• Usury is odious in law. [Exodus 22:25, Leviticus 25:36-37, Nehemiah 5:7,10, Proverbs 28:8, Ezekiel 18:8,13,17; 22:12]

Common Sense

• **When in doubt, do not act.**

• It is a fault to meddle with what does not belong to or does not concern you.

• Many men know many things, no one knows everything.

• **One is not present unless he understands.**

• It avails little to know what ought to be done, if you do not know **how** it is to be done.

• **He who questions well, learns well.**

• What ever is done in excess is prohibited by law.

• No one is bound to give information about things he is ignorant of, but every one is bound to know that which he gives information about.

• No man is bound to have foreknowledge of a Divine or a future event.

• No one is bound to arm his adversary.

Consent and Contracts

• Consent makes the law.

• A contract is a law between the parties, which can acquire force only by consent.

• Consent makes the law: the terms of a contract, lawful in its purpose, constitute the law as between the parties.

• To him consenting no injury is done.

• **He who consents cannot receive an injury.**

• Consent removes or obviates a mistake.

• He who mistakes is not considered as consenting.

• **Every consent involves a submission; but a mere submission does not necessarily involve consent.**

• A contract founded on a base and unlawful consideration, or against good morals, is null and void.

• One who wills a thing to be or to be done cannot complain of that thing as an injury.

• The agreement of the parties makes the law of the contract

• **The contract makes the law.**

• Agreements give the law to the contract

• The agreement of the parties prevails against the law

• Advice, unless fraudulent, does not create an obligation.

• No action arises out of an immoral consideration.

• No action arises on an immoral contract.

• In the agreements of the contracting parties, the rule is to regard the intention rather than the words.

• The right of survivorship does not exist among merchants for the benefit of commerce

• When two persons are liable on a joint obligation, if one makes default the other must bear the whole.

• **You ought to know with whom you deal.**

• He who contracts, knows, or ought to know, the quality

of the person with whom he contracts, otherwise he is not excusable.

• He who approves cannot reject.

• If anything is due to a corporation, it is not due to the individual members of it, nor do the members individually owe what the corporation owes.

• **Agreement takes the place of the law: the express understanding of parties supersedes such understanding as the law would imply.**

• Manner and agreement overrule the law.

• The essence of a contract being assent, there is no contract where assent is wanting.

Court and Pleas

• There can be no plea of that thing of which the dissolution is sought.

• A false plea is the basest of all things.

• There can be no plea against an action which entirely destroys the plea.

• **He who does not deny, admits.** [A well-known rule of pleading]

• No one is believed in court but upon his oath.

• An infamous person is repelled or prevented from taking an oath.

• In law none is credited unless he is sworn.

• All the facts must, when established by witnesses, be under oath or affirmation.

• An act of the court shall oppress no one.

• The practice of a court is the law of the court.

• There ought to be an end of law suits.

• It concerns the commonwealth that there be an end of law suits.

- It is for the public good that there be an end of litigation.
- A personal action dies with the person.
- This must be understood of an action for a tort only.
- Equity acts upon the person.
- **No one can sue in the name of another.**

Court Appearance

[This is why we should avoid voluntarily appearing in court]

- **A general appearance cures antecedent irregularity of process, a defective service, etc.**
- Certain legal consequences are attached to the voluntary act of a person.
- The presence of the body cures the error in the name; the truth of the name cures an error in the description
- An error in the name is immaterial if the body is certain.
- An error in the name is nothing when there is certainty as to the person.
- The truth of the demonstration removes the error of the name.

Crime and Punishment

- A madman is punished by his madness alone.
- The instigator of a crime is worse than he who perpetrates it.
- **They who consent to an act, and they who do it, shall be visited with equal punishment**
- Acting and consenting parties are liable to the same punishment.
- No one is punished for his thoughts
- **No one is punished for merely thinking of a crime.**
- He who has committed iniquity, shall not have equity.
- He who is once bad, is presumed to be always so in

the same degree.

• He who is once criminal is presumed to be always criminal in the same kind or way.

• Whatever is once bad, is presumed to be so always in the same degree.

• **He who does not forbid a crime while he may, sanctions it.**

• He who does not blame, approves.

• He is clear of blame who knows, but cannot prevent.

• **No one is to be punished for the crime or wrong of another.**

• **No guilt attaches to him who is compelled to obey.**

• Gross negligence is held equivalent to intentional wrong.

• Misconduct binds its own authors.

• It is a never-failing axiom that everyone is accountable only for his own offence or wrong.

• In offenses, the will and not the consequences are to be looked to.

• It is to the intention that all law applies.

• The intention of the party is the soul of the instrument.

• Every act is to be estimated by the intention of the doer.

• **An act does not make a man a criminal, unless his intention be criminal.**

• An act does not make a person guilty, unless the intention be also guilty. This maxim applies only to criminal cases; in civil matters it is otherwise.

• In offenses, the intention is regarded, not the event.

• The intention amounts to nothing unless some effect follows.

• Take away the will, and every action will be indifferent.

• Your motive gives a name to your act.

• An outlaw is put out of the protection of the law.

- Vainly does he who offends against the law, seek the help of the law.
- Drunkenness inflames and produces every crime.
- Drunkenness both aggravates and reveals every crime.
- He who sins when drunk shall be punished when sober.
- Punishment is due if the words of an oath be false.
- **A prison is established not for the sake of punishment, but of detention and guarding.**
- **Those sinning secretly are punished more severely than those sinning openly.**
- Punishment ought not to precede a crime.
- **If one falsely accuses another of a crime, the punishment due to that crime should be inflicted upon the perjured informer.** [Deuteronomy 19:18]

Customs and Usages

- **Long time and long use, beyond the memory of man, suffices for right.**
- Custom is the best expounder of the law.
- Custom is another law.
- A prescriptive and legitimate custom overcomes the law.
- **Custom leads the willing, law compels or draws the unwilling.**
- Usage is the best interpreter of things.
- Custom is the best interpreter of laws.
- What is done contrary to the custom of our ancestors, neither pleases nor appears right.
- Where two rights concur, the more ancient shall be preferred.

Expressions and Words

• **The meaning of words is the spirit of the law.** [Romans 8:2]

• The propriety of words is the safety of property.

• **It is immaterial whether a man gives his assent by words or by acts and deeds.**

• It matters not whether a revocation be by words or by acts.

• What is expressed renders what is implied silent.

• An unequivocal statement prevails over an implication.

• In ambiguous expressions, the intention of the person using them is chiefly to be regarded.

• The expression of those things which are tacitly implied operates nothing.

• The expression of one thing is the exclusion of another.

• A general expression is to be construed generally.

• A general expression implies nothing certain.

• General words are understood in a general sense.

• **When the words and the mind agree, there is no place for interpretation.**

• Every interpretation either declares, extends or restrains.

• **The best interpretation is made from things preceding and following; i.e., the context.**

• Words are to be interpreted according to the subject-matter.

• He who considers merely the letter of an instrument goes but skin deep into its meaning.

• Frequently where the propriety of words is attended to, the meaning of truth is lost.

• Words are to be taken most strongly against him who uses them.

• Multiplicity and indistinctness produce confusion; and questions, the more simple they are, the more lucid.

• When two things repugnant to each other are found in a will, the last is to be confirmed.

• Bad or false grammar does not vitiate a deed or grant.

• Many things can be implied from a few expressions.

• Language is the exponent of the intention.

• **Words are indicators of the mind or thought.**

• Speech is the index of the mind. [James 1:26]

• Laws are imposed, not upon words, but upon things.

Fictions

• A fiction is a rule of law that assumes something which is or may be false as true.

• **Where truth is, fiction of law does not exist.**

• There is no fiction without law.

• Fictions arise from the law, and not law from fictions.

• Fiction is against the truth, but it is to have truth.

• In a fiction of law, equity always subsists.

• **A fiction of law injures no one.**

• Fiction of law is wrongful if it works loss or injury to any one.

Fraud and Deceit

• **It is safer to be deceived than to deceive.**

• **A deceiver deals in generals.**

• Fraud lies hid in general expressions.

• A concealed fault is equal to a deceit

• Out of fraud no action arises.

• A forestaller is an oppressor of the poor, and a public enemy to the whole community and the country.

• It is a fraud to conceal a fraud.

• Gross negligence is equivalent to fraud.

• Once a fraud, always a fraud

• **What otherwise is good and just, if it be sought by force and fraud, becomes bad and unjust.**

• He is not deceived who knows himself to be deceived.

• Let him who wishes to be deceived, be deceived.

• He who does not prevent what he can, seems to commit the thing.

• He who does not prevent what he can prevent, is viewed as assenting.

• He who does not forbid what he can forbid, seems to assent

• He who does not forbid, when he might forbid, commands

• **He who does not repel a wrong when he can, induces it.**

• Often it is the new road, not the old one, which deceives the traveler.

• Deceit is an artifice, since it pretends one thing and does another.

God and Religion

• **If ever the law of God and man are at variance, the former are to be obeyed in derogation of the later.** [Acts 5:29]

• That which is against Divine Law is repugnant to society and is void.

• He who becomes a soldier of Christ has ceased to be a soldier of the world. [2 Timothy 2:3-4]

• Where the Divinity is insulted the case is unpardonable.

• Human things never prosper when divine things are neglected.

• No man is presumed to be forgetful of his eternal welfare, and particularly at the point of death.

• The church does not die.

• That is the highest law which favors religion.

• The law is from everlasting.

• He who acts badly, hates the light.

• He who does not willingly speak the truth, is a betrayer of the truth.

• **He who does not speak the truth, is a traitor to the truth.**

• The truth that is not sufficiently defended is frequently overpowered; and he who does not disapprove, approves.

• Suppression of the truth is equivalent to the expression of what is false.

• Truth, by whomever pronounced, is from God.

• Truth fears nothing but concealment.

• We can do nothing against truth. [2 Corinthians 13:

• Truth is the mother of justice.

• To swear is to call God to witness and is an act of religion.

• Earlier in time, is stronger in right.

• First in time, first in right.

• He who is before in time, is preferred in right.

• **What is first is truest; and what comes first in time, is best in law.**

• No man is ignorant of his eternal welfare.

• All men know God. [Hebrews 8:11]

• **The cause of the Church is a public cause.**

• **The Law of God and the law of the land are all one, and both favor and preserve the common good of the land.**

• No man warring for God should be troubled by secular business.

Governments and Jurisdiction

• **That which seems necessary for the king and the state ought not to be said to tend to the prejudice of liberty of the [Christ's] ekklesia.**

• **The power which is derived [from God] cannot be greater than that from which it is derived [God]**. [Romans 13:1]

• **The order of things is confounded if every one preserves not his jurisdiction [in and of Christ].**

• Jurisdiction is a power introduced for the public good, on account of the necessity of dispensing justice.

• Every jurisdiction has its own bounds.

• The government cannot confer a favor which occasions injury and loss to others.

• A minor ought not to be guardian of a minor, for he is unfit to govern others who does not know how to govern himself.

• The government is to be subject to the law, for the law makes government.

• The law is not to be violated by those in government.

Heirs

• **God, and not man, make the heir.** [Romans 8:16]

• God alone makes the heir, not man.

• Co-heirs are deemed as one body or person, by reason of the unity of right which they possess. [Romans 8:17, Ephesians 5:31-32]

• **No one can be both owner and heir at the same time.**

• An heir is either by right of property, or right of representation.

• An heir is the same person with his ancestor. [Because

the ancestor, during his life, bears in his body (of law) all his heirs].

• 'Heir' is a collective name or noun [so it is not private, and has no private rights].

• Several co-heirs are as one body, by reason of the unity of right which they possess. [Romans 8:17, Ephesians 5:31-32]

• The law favors a man's inheritance. Heir is a term of law, son one of nature. An heir is another self, and a son is a part of the father.

• The heir succeeds to the restitution not the penalty.

Judges and Judgment

• Let justice be done, though the heavens should fall.

• One who commands lawfully must be obeyed.

• **Whoever does anything by the command of a judge is not reckoned to have done it with an evil intent, because it is necessary to obey.** [Isaiah 33:22, "For the LORD is our judge…"]

• Where a person does an act by command of one exercising judicial authority, the law will not suppose that he acted from any wrongful or improper motive, because it was his bounden duty to obey.

• A judgment is always taken as truth. If you judge, understand.

• It is the duty of a good judge to remove the cause of litigation. [Acts 18:12-16]

• The end of litigation is justice.

• To a judge who exceeds his office or jurisdiction no obedience is due.

• One who exercises jurisdiction out of his territory is not obeyed with impunity.

• A twisting of language is unworthy of a judge.

• A good judge decides according to justice and right, and prefers equity to strict law.

• Of the credit and duty of a judge, no question can arise; but it is otherwise respecting his knowledge, whether he be mistaken as to the law or fact.

• It is punishment enough for a judge that he is responsible to God. [Psalms 2:10-12, Romans 13]

• That is the best system of law which confides as little as possible to the discretion of the judge.

• That law is the best which leaves the least discretion to the judge; and this is an advantage which results from certainty.

• He is the best judge who relies as little as possible on his own discretion.

• Whenever there is a doubt between liberty and slavery, the decision must be in favor of liberty.

• He who decides anything, a party being unheard, though he should decide right, does wrong.

• He who spares the guilty, punishes the innocent. [Mark 15:6-15, Luke 23:17-25, John 18:38-40]

• The judge is condemned when a guilty person escapes punishment.

• What appears not does not exist, and nothing appears judicially before judgment.

• It is improper to pass an opinion on any part of a sentence, without examining the whole.

• Hasty justice is the step-mother of misfortune. Faith is the sister of justice.

• Justice knows not father not mother; justice looks at truth alone.

• **A judge is not to act upon his personal judgment**

or from a dictate of private will, but to pronounce according to law and justice.
- No one should be judge in his own cause.
- No one can be at once judge and party.
- **A judge is to expound, not to make, the law.**
- It is the duty of a judge to declare the law, not to enact the law or make it.
- Definite, legal conclusions cannot be arrived at upon hypothetical averments.
- A judge is the law speaking. [the mouth of the law]
- A judge should have two salts: the salt of wisdom, lest he be insipid; and the salt of conscience, lest he be devilish.
- **He who flees judgment confesses his guilt.**
- No man should be condemned unheard. The judge is counsel for the prisoner.
- Everyone is presumed to be innocent until his guilt is established beyond a reasonable doubt.
- Justice is neither to be denied nor delayed.
- It is the property of a Judge to administer justice, not to give it.
- Justice is an excellent virtue, and pleasing to the Most High.

Law
- A maxim is so called because its dignity is chiefest, and its authority most certain, and because universally approved of all.
- **All law has either been derived from the consent of the people, established by necessity, confirmed by custom, or of Divine Providence.**
- Nothing is so becoming to authority [God] as to live according to the law [of God].

• **He acts prudently who obeys the commands of the Law.** [Ecclesiastes 12:13]

• Law is the safest helmet; under the shield of the law no one is deceived. [Ephesians 6:13-17, 1 Thessalonians 5:8]

• An argument drawn from authority [scripture] is the strongest in law.

• An argument drawn from a similar case, or analogy, avails in law.

• That which was originally void, does not by lapse of time become valid.

• The law does not seek to compel a man to do that which he cannot possibly perform.

• The law requires nothing impossible.

• **The law compels no one to do anything which is useless or impossible.**

• No one is bound to do what is impossible. Impossibility excuses the law.

• No prescription runs against a person unable to act.

• The law shall not, through the medium of its executive capacity, work a wrong.

• The law does wrong to no one. An act of the law wrongs no man.

• The law never works an injury, or does him a wrong.

• The construction of law works not an injury.

• An argument drawn from what is inconvenient is good in law, because the law will not permit any inconvenience.

• Nothing inconvenient is lawful.

• Nothing against reason is lawful.

• **The law which governs corporations is the same as that which governs individuals.**

• Nothing against reason is lawful.

• The laws sometimes sleep, but never die.

- A contemporaneous exposition is the best and most powerful in the law.
- The law never suffers anything contrary to truth.
- Law is the dictate of reason.
- The law does not notice or care for trifling matters.
- **It is a miserable slavery where the law is vague or uncertain.**
- It is a wretched state of things when the law is vague and mutable.
- Examples illustrate and do not restrict the law.
- The disposition of law is firmer and more powerful than the will of man.
- Law is established for the benefit of man. [Mark 2:27]
- To be able to know is the same as to know.
- This maxim is applied to the duty of every one to know the law.
- We may do what is allowed by law.
- Ignorance of fact may excuse, but not ignorance of law.
- Ignorance of facts excuses, ignorance of law does not excuse.
- In a doubtful case, that is the construction of the law which the words indicate.
- In doubt, the gentler course is to be followed.
- In doubt, the safer course is to be adopted.
- In a deed which may be considered good or bad, the law looks more to the good than to the bad.
- In things favored what does good is more regarded than what does harm.
- In all affairs, and principally in those which concern the administration of justice, the rules of equity ought to be followed.
- In ambiguous things, such a construction is to be made,

that what is inconvenient and absurd is to be avoided.
- Law is the science of what is good and evil.
- **The law punishes falsehood.**
- Reason and authority are the two brightest lights in the world.
- The reason of the law is the soul of the law.
- The reason ceasing, the law itself ceases.
- When the reason, which is the soul of a law, ceases to exist, the law itself should lose its operative effect.
- **and die. It is a perpetual law that no human or positive law can be perpetual.**
- If you depart from the law you will wander without a guide and everything will be in a state of uncertainty to every one. [Joshua 1:8]
- Where there is no law there is no transgression, as it regards the world. [Romans 4:15]
- Everything is permitted, which is not forbidden by law.
- All rules of law are liable to exceptions. [Matthew 12:1-5]
- What is inconvenient or contrary to reason, is not allowed in law.
- The laws serve the vigilant, not those who sleep upon their rights.
- Relief is not given to such as sleep on their rights.
- Nothing unjust is presumed in law. Acts required by law to be done, admit of no qualification.
- To know the laws, is not to observe their mere words, but their force and power. [John 6:68]
- We are all bound to our lawgiver, regardless of our personal interpretation of reality. [Isaiah 33:22, James 4:12]
- Legality is not reality The law sustains the watchful.
- Those awake, not those asleep, the laws assist. [1

Timothy 1:9]

• Legal remedies are for the active and vigilant. What is good and equal, is the law of laws.

• Whose right it is to institute, his right it is to abrogate.

• **Laws are abrogated or repealed by the same authority by which they are made.**

• The civil law is what a people establishes for itself. [It is not established by God]

• Many things have been introduced into the common law, with a view to the public good, which are inconsistent with sound reason. [The law of merchants was merged with the common law]

• The people is the greatest master of error.

• **A man may obey the law and yet be neither honest nor a good neighbor.**

• To investigate [inquire into] is the way to know what things are truly lawful. [2 Timothy 2:15]

• Those who do not preserve the law of the land, they justly incur the awesome and indelible brand of infamy.

• An exception to the rule should not destroy the rule.

• Laws should bind their own maker.

• **Necessity overrules the law.**

• Necessity makes that lawful which otherwise is not lawful.

• Things which are tolerated on account of necessity ought not to be drawn into precedents.

• **It has been said, with much truth, "Where the law ends, tyranny begins."**

Marriage

• The law favors dower; it is the reward of chastity; therefore let it be preserved. [Exodus 22:17]

• **Husband and wife are considered one person in law.** [Genesis 2:24]
  • A wife is not her own mistress, but is under the power of her husband.
  • The union of a man and a woman is of the law of nature.
  • Marriages ought to be free.
  • All things which are of the wife, belong to the husband. [Genesis 3:16]
  • Although the property may be the wife's, the husband is the keeper of it, since he is the head of the wife.
  • **Consent, and not cohabitation, makes the marriage.**
  • Insanity prevents marriage from being contracted, because consent is needed.
  • A wife follows the domicile of her husband.
  • Husband and wife cannot be a witness for, or against, each other, because of the union of person that exists.
  • The right of blood and kindred cannot be destroyed by any civil law. [Acts 17:26-28]
  • Children are the blood of their parents, but the father and mother are not of the blood of the children.

Miscellaneous
  • He who has the risk has the dominion or advantage.
  • There is no disputing against a man denying principles.
  • The immediate, and not the remote cause, is to be considered.
  • A consequence ought not to be drawn from another consequence.
  • He who takes away the means, destroys the end
  • He who destroys the means, destroys the end.
  • He who seeks a reason for everything, subverts reason.

- Every exception not watched tends to assume the place of the principle.
- Where there is a right, there is a remedy.
- For every legal right the law provides a remedy.
- He who uses the right of another [belonging to Christ] ought to use the same right [of Christ]. [In other words, don't use something new, or something outside of Christ].
- Liberty is an inestimable good.
- All shall have liberty to renounce those things which have been established in their favor.
- Power is not conferred, but for the public good.
- Power ought to follow, not to precede justice.
- To know properly is to know the reason and cause of a thing.
- **The useful by the useless is not destroyed.**
- Where there is no act, there can be no force.
- One may not do an act to himself.
- A thing done cannot be undone.
- No man is bound for the advice he gives.
- He who commands a thing to be done is held to have done it himself.
- **When anything is commanded, everything by which it can be accomplished is also commanded.**
- The principal part of everything is the beginning.
- To refer errors to their origin is to refute them. The origin of a thing ought to be inquired into.
- **Human nature does not change with time or environment.**
- Anger is short insanity.
- It is lawful to repel force by force, provided it be done with the moderation of blameless defense, not for the purpose of taking revenge, but to ward off injury.

- **The status of a person is his legal position or condition.**
- A person is a man considered with reference to a certain status.
- The partner of my partner is not my partner.
- Use is the master of things, experience is the mistress of things.
- **Protection draws to it subjection, subjection, protection.**
- Error artfully colored is in many things more probable than naked truth; and frequently error conquers truth and reasoning.

Officers

- **Ignorance of the Law does not excuse misconduct in anyone, least of all a sworn officer of the law.**
- Summonses or citations should not be granted before it is expressed under the circumstances whether the summons ought to be made.
- A delegated power cannot be again delegated.
- A deputy cannot appoint a deputy.
- An office ought to be injurious to no one.
- A neglected duty often works as much against the interests as a duty wrongfully performed.
- Failure to enforce the law does not change it.
- It is contrary to the Law of Nations to do violence to Ambassadors.
- **An Ambassador fills the place of the king by whom he is sent, and is to be honored as he is whose place he fills.**
- The greatest enemies to peace are force and wrong. Force and wrong are greatly contrary to peace. Force is

inimical [hostile] to the law.

Possession
• No one gives who does not have.
• **No one can give what he does not own.**
• One cannot transfer to another a right which he has not.
• He gives nothing who has nothing.
• Two cannot possess one thing each in entirety.
• A gift is rendered complete by the possession of the receiver.
• What is mine cannot be taken away without my consent.
• He that gives never ceases to possess until he that receives begins to possess.
• **A person in possession is not bound to prove that the possessions belong to him.**
• Things taken or captured by pirates and robbers do not change their ownership.
• Things which are taken from enemies immediately become the property of the captors.
• **It is one thing to possess, it is another to be in possession.**
• Possession of the termer, possession of the reversioner.

Property and Land
• Land lying unoccupied is given to the first occupant.
• What belongs to no one, naturally belong to the first occupant.
• Possession is a good title, where no better title appears.
• **Long possession produces the right of possession, and takes away from the true owner his action.**
• When a man has the possession as well as the right of

property, he is said to have *jus duplicatum* - a double right, forming a complete title.

• **Rights of dominion are transferred without title or delivery, by prescription, *to wit*, long and quiet possession.**

• Possessor has right against all men but him who has the very right.

• Enjoy your own property in such a manner as not to injure that of another person.

• He who owns the soil, owns up to the sky.

• **The owner of a piece of land owns everything above and below it to an indefinite extent.**

• Of whom is the land, of him is it also to the sky and to the deepest depths; he who owns the land owns all above and all below the surface.

• Every person has exclusive dominion over the soil which he absolutely owns; hence such an owner of land has the exclusive right of hunting and fishing on his land, and the waters covering it.

• Every man's house is his castle.

• A citizen cannot be taken by force from his house to be conducted before a judge or to prison.

• The habitation of each one is an inviolable asylum for him.

• Whatever is affixed to the soil belongs to it.

• Rivers and ports are public, therefore the right of fishing there is common to all.

• Land comprehends any ground soil, or earth whatsoever; as meadows, pastures, woods, moors, waters, and marshes.

Right and Wrong

• A right cannot arise from a wrong.

• You are not to do evil that good may come of it.

• **It is not lawful to do evil that good may come of it.**

• That interpretation is to be received, which will not intend a wrong.

• It is better to suffer every wrong, than to consent to it.

• **It is better to recede than to proceed wrongly.**

• To lie is to go against the mind.

• The multitude of those who err is no excuse for error. [Exodus 23:2]

• No one is considered as committing damages, unless he is doing what he has no right to do.

• No one shall take advantage of his own wrong.

• No man ought to derive any benefit of his own wrong. No one ought to gain by another's loss.

• No one ought to enrich himself at the expense of others.

• No one can improve his condition by a crime.

• He who uses his legal rights, harms no one.

• **An error not resisted is approved.**

• He who is silent appears to consent.

• Things silent are sometimes considered as expressed.

• To conceal is one thing, to be silent another.

• **Concealment of the truth is (equivalent to) a statement of what is false.**

• Suppression of fact, which should be disclosed, is the same in effect as willful misrepresentation.

• Evil is not presumed. It is safer to err on the side of mercy.

Scriptural

• **Unequal things ought not to be joined.** [2 Corinthians 6:14]

   • Things unite with similar things.

   • The law is no respecter of persons. [Acts 10:34]

   • Time runs against the slothful and those who neglect their rights. [Proverbs 24:30-31]

   • Debts follow the person of the debtor.

• **The most favorable construction is made in restitutions.** [Exodus 22:5-6,12]

   • Where damages are given, the losing party should pay the costs of the victor.

• **In many counselors there is safety.** [Proverbs 11:14; 15:22; 24:6]

• **Remove the foundation, the structure or work fall.** [Luke 6:48-49]

   • A legacy is confirmed by the death of the testator, in the same manner as a gift from a living person is by delivery alone. [Hebrews 9:16]

   • The will of a testator is ambulatory (alterable, revocable) up to his death. [Hebrews 9:16-17]

   • Every will is completed at death. A will speaks from the time of death only. [Hebrews 9:16-17]

   • The last will of a testator is to be fulfilled according to his real intention.

   • To insult the deity is an unpardonable offense. [Matthew 12:31]

   • Women are excluded from all civil and public charges or offices. [1 Timothy 2:12, 1 Corinthians 14:34].

   • He who is in the womb, is considered as born, whenever it is for his benefit. [Job 31:15, Isaiah 49:1,5, Jeremiah 1:5]

   • He who first offends, causes the strife. [Matthew 5:22]

• He who pays tardily, pays less than he ought. [Leviticus 19:13, Deuteronomy 24:14-15]

• **The beaten path is the safe path; the old way is the safe way.** [Jeremiah 6:16]

Servants and Slaves

• Whatever is acquired by the servant, is acquired for the master.

• **A slave is not a person.**

• **A slave, and everything a slave has, belongs to his master.**

• He who acts by or through another, acts for himself.

• He who does anything through another, is considered as doing it himself.

• The master is liable for injury done by his servant.

• **He is not presumed to consent who obeys the orders of his father or his master.**

Wisdom and Knowledge

• If you know not the names of things, the knowledge of things themselves perishes; and of you lose the names, the distinction of the things is certainly lost.

• Names are mutable, but things immutable.

• Names of things ought to be understood according to common usage, not according to the opinions of individuals.

• A name is not sufficient if a thing or subject for it does not exist by law or by fact.

• Not to believe rashly is the nerve of wisdom.

• Reason is a ray of the Divine Light. [Isaiah 1:18]

• Abundant caution does no harm.

• External acts indicate undisclosed thoughts.

• **Outward acts evince the inward purpose.**

• **You will perceive many things more easily by practice than by rules.**

• Remove the cause and the effect will cease.

• **Give the things which are yours whilst they are yours; after death they are not yours.**

Witnesses and Proof

• A witness is a person who is present at and observes a transaction.

• **The answer of one witness shall not be heard.** [Deuteronomy 19:15]

• The testimony of one witness, unsupported, may not be enough to convict; for there may then be merely oath against oath.

• This is a maxim of the civil law, where everything must be proved by two witnesses. [Matthew 18:16, 2 Corinthians 13:1]

• In law, none is credited unless he is sworn.

• All facts must, when established by witnesses, be under oath or affirmation.

• **A confession made in court is of greater effect than any proof.**

• No man is bound to produce writings against himself.

• No one can be made to testify against himself or betray himself.

• No one is bound to accuse himself.

• No one ought to accuse himself, unless before God.

• One making a voluntary confession, is to be dealt with more mercifully.

• He ought not to be heard who advances a proposition contrary to the rules of law.

• False in one (particular), false in all.

- Deliberate falsehood in one matter will be imputed to related matters.
- **He who alleges contradictory things is not to be listened to.**
- Proofs are to be weighed not numbered; that is, the more worthy or credible are to be believed.
- It doesn't matter how many men say something, because the Word of God is superior to all.
- It does not matter how many people believe a lie, it's still a lie. And in a democracy, a lie is the truth].
- **A presumption will stand good until the contrary is proved.**
- The presumption is always in favor of the one who denies.
- All things are presumed to be lawfully done and duly performed until the contrary is proved.
- When the plaintiff does not prove his case, the defendant is absolved.
- When opinions are equal, a defendant is acquitted.
- **An act done by me against my will is not my act.**
- What does not appear and what is not is the same; it is not the defect of law, but the want of proof.
- The faculty or right of offering proof is not to be narrowed.
- The latter decisions are stronger in law.
- No one is restrained from using several defenses.
- No one is bound to inform about a thing he knows not, but he who gives information is bound to know what he says.
- No one is bound to expose himself to misfortune and dangers.
- Plain truths need not be proved.
- What is clearly apparent need not be proved.
- One eye witness is better than ten ear ones.

- An eye witness outweighs others.
- What appears to the court needs not the help of witnesses.
- It is in the nature of things, that he who denies a fact is not bound to prove it.
- The burden of proof lies upon him who affirms, not on him who denies.
- The claimant is always bound to prove: the burden of proof lies on him.
- **Upon the one alleging, not upon him denying, rests the duty of proving.**
- Upon the plaintiff rests the proving – the burden of proof.
- The necessity of proving lies with him who makes the charge.
- When the law presumes the affirmative, the negative is to be proved.
- When the proofs of facts are present, what need is there of words.
- **It is vain to prove that which if proved would not aid the matter in question.**
- Facts are more powerful than words.
- Negative facts are not proof.
- Witnesses cannot testify to a negative; they must testify to an affirmative.
- Better is the condition of the defendant, than that of the plaintiff.
- **What is not proved and what does not exist are the same; it is not a defect of the law, but of proof.**
- Principles prove, they are not proved.
- There is no reasoning of principles.
- All things are presumed to have been done in due and solemn form.

BE THE ONE

Closing thoughts

Your word is indeed enough. **But most do not h**ave the capacity to state clearly who they are when confronted and will cave in the first time they are dragged into court.

It is as simple as not giving that trooper your drivers license when you are not involved in commerce and you are not required to do so. But how many will *not comply* and ask him to identify himself first.

It is at this point that I hand him My picture ID with a warning clearly stated on the back as Notice to him that it will cost him to detain me when he has no jurisdiction.

My picture ID has my *given name,* not my strawman name that they presume to own and enslave.

Anyone can do it whatsoever way they wish; this is just the way I do it.

If you want to go to court then use your enslavement government ID, otherwise you need to Notice the agent, trooper, or whoever, of your status as a Sovereign Nation State from the beginning of any encounter.

When in the Public, you have to be prepared to act as they expect. To me that means identify yourself if required.

In most cases it is not required, and you cannot be made to, but you could then end up in jail for 72 hours until they identify you.

They tried that on a native woman here and jailed her as a "Jane Doe", and while she was in jail they went thru her stuff and found a drivers license and took it to her and said: Is this you? She said "Are you nuts do I look like a piece of plastic to you"?

They finally let her go because she would not identify with the strawperson identity.

On another occasion she was jailed for digging clams; when she went to court she took a basket with a straw figure in it with the drivers license, registration and other papers and said: "I am here for that matter and I have SHARON with me. Sharon is property of the state, and I have her here to turn her over to you" — again they let her go.

So it all comes down to Status and Who you are; knowing who you are, and if needed, defending who you are. Some can do that, others cannot.

BE THE ONE

Other Publications

NESARA I & II: National Economic Security
and Reformation Act
I: http://tinyurl.com/c8u42q6
II: http://tinyurl.com/848mqag

History of Banking: An Asian Perspective
http://tinyurl.com/7oxjwft

The People's Voice: Former Arizona
Sheriff Richard Mack
http://tinyurl.com/d62fyg3

Asset Protection: Pure Trust Organizations
http://tinyurl.com/btrjfqp

The Matrix As It Is: A Different Point Of View
http://tinyurl.com/87pbtom

From Debt To Prosperity: 'Social Credit' Defined
http://tinyurl.com/c4r577x

Give Yourself Credit: Money Doesn't Grow On Trees
http://tinyurl.com/d9mf5yt

My Home Is My Castle: Beware Of The Dog
http://tinyurl.com/bmzxc2n

Commercial Redemption: The Hidden Truth
http://tinyurl.com/d9etg7w

Hardcore Redemption-In-Law: Commercial Freedom And
Release
http://tinyurl.com/cl65vrz

Oil Beneath Our Feet: America's Energy Non-Crisis
http://tinyurl.com/btlzqxf

Untold History Of America: Let The Truth Be Told
http://tinyurl.com/bu9kjjc

Debtocracy: & Odious Debt Explained
http://tinyurl.com/cooqzuz

New Beginning Study Course: Connect The Dots And See
http://tinyurl.com/cxpk42p

Monitions of a Mountain Man: Manna, Money, & Me
http://tinyurl.com/cusgcqs

Maine Street Miracle: Saving Yourself And America
http://tinyurl.com/d4yktlw

Reclaim Your Sovereignty: Take Back Your Christian Name
http://tinyurl.com/cf5taxh

Gun Carry In The USA: Your Right To Self-defence
http://tinyurl.com/cdn3y3y

Climategate Debunked: Big Brother, Main Stream Media
http://tinyurl.com/d6gy2xz

Epistle to the Americans I: What you don't
know about The Income Tax
http://tinyurl.com/d99ujzm

Epistle to the Americans II: What you don't
know about American History
http://tinyurl.com/cnyghyz

Epistle to the Americans III: What you don't
know about Money
http://tinyurl.com/cp8nrh8